AND TOOLS

SOLO

free agent manual

the land of the free is a state of mind

Josephine Monroe

momentum

www.yourmomentum.com

the stuff that drives you

What is momentum?

Momentum is a completely new publishing philosophy, in print and online, dedicated to giving you more of the information, inspiration and drive to enhance who you are, what you do, and how you do it.

Fusing the changing forces of work, life and technology, momentum will give you the right stuff for a brighter future and set you on the way to being all you can be.

Who needs momentum?

Momentum is for people who want to make things happen in their careers and their lives, who want to work at something they enjoy and that's worthy of their talents and their time. Momentum people have values and principles, and question who they are, what they do, and who for. Wherever they work, they want to feel proud of what they do. And they are hungry for information, stimulation, ideas and answers …

Momentum online

Visit *www.yourmomentum.com* to be part of the talent community. Here you'll find a full listing of current and future books, an archive of articles by momentum authors, sample chapters and self-assessment tools. While you're there, post your work/life questions to our momentum coaches and sign up to receive free newsletters with even more stuff to drive you.

More momentum

If you need more drive for your life, try one of these other momentum titles:

soultrader
personal career strategies for life
Carmel McConnell

reinvent yourself
tactics for work, life and happiness – yours
J. Jonathan Gabay

mental space
how to find clarity in a complex life
Tina Konstant and Morris Taylor

be your own career consultant
work out where you want to be – and get there
Gary Pyke and Stuart Neath

managing brand me
how to build your personal brand
Thomas Gad and Anette Rosencreutz

coach yourself
make real change in your life
Anthony M. Grant and Jane Greene

change activist
make big things happen fast
Carmel McConnell

lead yourself
be where others will follow
Mick Cope

happy mondays
putting the pleasure back into work
Richard Reeves

the big difference
life works when you choose it
Nicola Phillips

hey you!
pitch to win in an ideas economy
Will Murray

snap, crackle or stop
change your career and create your own destiny
Barbara Quinn

float you
how to capitalize on your talent
Carmel McConnell and Mick Cope

from here to e
equip yourself for a career in the wired economy
Lisa Khoo

grow your personal capital
what you know, who you know and how you use it
Hilarie Owen

PEARSON EDUCATION LIMITED

Head Office:
Edinburgh Gate
Harlow CM20 2JE
Tel: +44 (0)1279 623623
Fax: +44 (0)1279 431059

London Office:
128 Long Acre
London WC2E 9AN
Tel: +44 (0)20 7447 2000
Fax: +44 (0)20 7447 2170
Website: www.yourmomentum.com

First published in Great Britain in 2002

ISBN 1843 040212

British Library Cataloguing in Publication Data
A CIP catalogue record for this book can be obtained from the British Library.

10 9 8 7 6 5 4 3 2 1

Typeset by Northern Phototypesetting Co. Ltd, Bolton
Printed and bound in Great Britain by Henry Ling Ltd, Dorchester
Cover and concept design by Heat
Production design by Claire Brodmann Book Designs, Lichfield, Staffs

The Publishers' policy is to use paper manufactured from sustainable forests.

dedication ...

to Julian Bovis

grounding

part one
the rules

part two
the tools

grounding

This section of the book will help you understand what free agency is all about – where it came from, what the benefits are and if it's right for you

chapter one
what is free agency?

It's not what you do, it's the way that you do it

A Free Agent can work for a salary. A Free Agent can run their own business. Or be freelance. Or be a student. Or do voluntary work. A Free Agent is not defined by what they do, but rather by the way that they do it.

Throughout this book you will read profiles of Free Agents who earn their income in a myriad of ways. Some Free Agents are PAYE employees, others earn just some of their money PAYE. Some charge by the hour, another uses the internet to sell the goods he makes in his garage. One makes money by selling his home every year to make a profit while another borrowed money to fund a course of study that will benefit them in the long run.

The qualities these people have in common are what make them Free Agents and what made them able to be Free Agents in the first place: independent thinking, self-belief, bravery, imagination and sound financial knowledge. The benefits they share are what will make Free Agency the dominant work pattern of the twenty-first century: satisfaction, flexibility and financial freedom. This book will give you the rules and the tools you need to become a successful Free Agent.

Whether you are currently freelance, employed or self-employed, this book can help you reap the financial and emotional rewards of taking responsibility for the way you earn money. Note the language here – we're no longer talking in terms of jobs, or even work. Free Agency is about your ability to earn money in the way that gives you greatest pleasure.

And the beauty of Free Agency is that – as you are now your own boss, *whoever you work for* – you get to define what gives you pleasure. If your priority is freeing up time to spend with your kids or on your garden, then Free Agency will give you that time. If your idea of pleasure is an early retirement to a villa overlooking the Mediterranean, then get in the queue for visas to Free Agent Nation. If it's important to you that the work you do marries with your ethics and values, then by assuming responsibility for the next steps you take in your life, Free Agency will deliver on that front too.

Free Agency is talent in exchange for opportunity.

This is the simplest definition of Free Agency there is. You decide to give your time / talent / energy / etc. in exchange for an opportunity to earn money / make contacts / learn new skills / etc.

Like all great laws of physics and commerce, this one is also universal. It applies to everyone and every industry. It applies to those who are still at school and those who have long retired. Free Agency suits gung-ho twenty-somethings scrambling for City millions and seventy-somethings who realize their knowledge and skills still command a decent price. This is a trend we will all become aware of in the next few decades: as university degrees become commonplace and no longer mark out graduates as desirable, we will enter the job market younger perhaps via apprenticeships or other vocational training. And as the population ages, we will all be forced to earn money long after what is currently considered 'pensionable age'.

So if we're all going to work for 70 years instead of the twentieth-century norm of 40–45 years, we had better make sure that we enjoy what we do. While few of us will realize childhood dreams to fly

e a movie star, most of us can – at any stage in our lives –
d deliver greater satisfaction for ourselves. We can be
ts, happier sales execs, happier plumbers. Free
y to this.

gency lends itself to traditionally creative and flexible essions: the media has long relied on contributors and eelancers; Hollywood signs up actors and key grips for individual films; and publishers sign up authors by the book.

But it's not just the media and creative professions where you find Free Agents. Increasingly, other sectors rely on contract, contingency and temporary staff. Banking, engineering, retail and manufacturing are all in need of competent people to work on individual contracts. At the same time there is a fundamental and radical change going on in the way that people think about work. Individuals no longer consider themselves as having jobs for life. Increasingly, people are taking more responsibility for their own career development and the balance of work and home life they want to achieve during their careers. It's here that the seeds for Free Agency are sown.

Brook Street, the High Street temp agency, summed up this new attitude to work in a recent advertising campaign on the London Underground with slogans like 'You are your own business. Me plc doesn't owe its existence to any employer' and 'The job for life is dead. Send no flowers.' The campaign hit home, prompting a 50 per cent increase in applications and a comparable rise in new client briefs.

A finger in every pie

If you were to go to a financial adviser to talk about planning for your financial future, he or she would almost certainly recommend taking a 'portfolio' approach to your fund. You should buy shares in a couple of FTSE 100 blue-chip companies, maybe the odd high-risk start-up to bring the chance of spectacular growth, some tracker bonds that keep your fund performing at the general rate of the stock market as a whole. And if you're a football fan, you might want to stick a few hundred quid on the old club for sentimental reasons. At least your investment here will always keep you interested.

Now, if you took a similar approach to *earning* money as you did to *investing* it, you would see in an instant how earning your money from a variety of sources makes sound financial sense.

You might have a contract with one employer for a fixed amount of work each month on a retainer. You might then do a couple of one-off jobs every now and then at a higher rate. You might spend some time putting a pitch together for a contract you might not get, but if you did, it could bring you enough money to take a month off. You might even work for free for a start-up in exchange for a small amount of equity that will bring you either money or knowledge – in Free Agent Nation both will make you rich.

It seems impossible to many people in traditional PAYE jobs that their company may get rid of them or may simply cease to exist. But if you stop and think for a minute, how many of the companies you have worked for still exist? In these days of multi-billion-dollar mergers and takeovers, even jobs in giant corporations aren't safe. Most of us will outlive the corporations we work for. And as those multi-billion-dollar corporations are run by accountants, your job may not be as safe as you think. Your boss may love the work you do, but what happens if she is laid off by one of those accountants? How safe do you feel now?

Quite simply, portfolio earning is the most sensible approach to take. This book will help you find out what pies you should be putting your fingers in, while making sure that at least one of them is a plum!

Some of the advice in this book will be more applicable to freelancers, other pieces will be more relevant to staffers – it depends which sort of pie you've got your finger in at this particular time. However, as a Free Agent, the rest of your working days are likely to be a mix of PAYE time, freelance time and contract time, so it should all be relevant to you at some point.

But I'm scared!

While the theory is sound, in practice leaving a 'safe' job for a world of invoices, self-assessment tax returns and months when the cheques just don't arrive is daunting, if not frightening. But as the Americans are very good at saying, 'No risk, no reward'. Don't think of the negatives (this book will take care of them anyway), instead accentuate the positives. Free Agency puts you in control, makes you an equal with whoever pays your salary, gives you self-esteem, and rewards you for initiative and industry.

Free Agency is a fair day's pay for a fun day's work

In addition to the rational fears of privation, starvation and loneliness (and you know it can't be *that* bad!) there is the emotional fear too. Successful Free Agency requires you to take responsibility for your actions, and not everyone is grown up enough to do that. You will no longer be able to blame your boss, your co-worker or the markets for your lack of work/success/money. Free Agency is about being smart and capitalizing on the opportunities created by not working solely for one employer. Blaming other people is a safety-net you are going to have to work without from now on. It may be frightening, but it shouldn't be. You're an adult. And you're smart. You know it's ridiculous that so many people never actually take charge of their future. So don't be dumb – set yourself free. As the Americans also say, 'Sometimes you just gotta feel the fear and do it anyway.'

What Free Agency is not

It's worth pointing out at this point – before you read any further – what Free Agency is not. It is not a quick fix, a gimmick or a fad. This book does not contain any scams, shortcuts or tricks for a fast buck or an early retirement. It's not about surfing while no one's looking or long lunches on somebody else's expense account. It's about being good at what you do and getting paid well for your time, knowledge and ability.

chapter two
where did free agents come from?

From the land of giants

There have, of course, always been Free Agents, long before the term was coined. Plumbers and tradesmen, journalists and actors, people running businesses from home have all effectively been Free Agenting for decades. Only it used to be called self-employed.

What made Free Agency an economic phenomenon, however, were the changes to employment practice which began with massive lay-offs and downsizing in the 1980s. It was a time when highly qualified and experienced professionals found themselves with a nice redundancy pay-off in their pockets and little chance of finding salaried work again. As companies looked for younger (i.e. cheaper) workers, older professionals set up consultancies and moved from the land of giant corporations to Free Agent Nation.

At the same time in the 1980s and early 1990s, the unions were crushed in industries as diverse as mining and publishing. Big companies got rid of staff members, and the associated commitments to pay health cover, National Insurance contributions, pension contributions, holiday pay, etc. They replaced them with contractors and freelancers, people who were paid by the day, the hour, or the job.

It signalled the end of the corporate career. The idea that a bright young thing out of school or university would join a firm in a junior role and wait to be promoted by meaningless increments until he or she retired was now ridiculous. The paternal service many companies had long provided for their workers was being withdrawn.

Corporate literacy

As we moved into the 1990s, workers realized that the bad news might have been that the job for life was dead, but the good news was that, hey, the job for life was dead. Not only did employers not have to subsidize their employees' pensions, but employees themselves no longer had to subsidize their co-workers' pensions either. Fast, efficient employees no longer got paid the same as useless and lazy employees; the childless no longer subsidized their co-workers' parental leave. Working under the new rules, good workers could get paid more or work fewer hours for the same money.

The Job for Life is dead. Long live Free Agent Nation!

In addition to earning more per hour, workers no longer had a sense of responsibility to their employer, who could no longer command authority because there was no fat leaving pension waiting in the future. So instead of weekend conferences being an imposition made by bosses on their workers, they became opportunities to network and to get head-hunted. Job tenure rates dropped dramatically, forcing employees to take out private pensions, private healthcare insurance, etc. Thatcher's children had already lost hope that the state would provide for them and were already warmed up to such changes.

This in turn meant that more and more of us became interested in the performance of the stock market. Suddenly our own pensions and investments were calculable – and we paid attention. The pagination of business sections of newspapers grew, investment magazines sprung up for the general consumer, and business stories started becoming headline news. Power had shifted from Westminster to the City.

Add to this the dotcom frenzy around the turn of the century when vast fortunes were won (and lost) in a short space of time, and it's no wonder that more and more of us found out how businesses worked. Consequently, the number of MBA courses on offer in the UK increased a hundred-fold from 1980 levels. Sales of business books rose as workers educated themselves with new skills and more knowledge.

The rise in corporate literacy is a key factor in the rise of Free Agency as well as a factor in the success of many Free Agents. A basic understanding of supply and demand, markets and best practice underlies any successful operator's specialist knowledge.

Corporate mercenaries

While many Free Agents had no choice but to fly solo, others left jobs of their own free will to become corporate mercenaries, guns for hire who would do any job if the price was right.

For some, becoming a parent was the catalyst that made them change the routine of commuting and working late. For others the sheer tedium and general hell of commuting through increasingly busy cities provided the motivation to start working from the loft. Others simply started to find their jobs less and less appealing as memo after memo asked them to cut costs and save time. And for younger Agents, being freelance or willing to work on contract was the only way to get a toe in the door of a coveted profession.

The rise in corporate literacy itself was the catalyst for many – they looked around at the world of business and saw that employees never got rich. For others who had previously found status and self-worth from their jobs, the time to leave came when MBA graduates were lured to their corporations with ridiculous and meaningless job titles like Vice-President of Expansion, or Director of New Business

Development. If they were motivated by status, they had just been seriously undermined, and so many chose to become the Chief Executive of Me plc.

Free Agency is undoubtedly a phenomenon of excess. It has grown out of decades of post-war prosperity among those who no longer live in fear of – or are incapable of comprehending – poverty, hunger and destitution. With our primal survival needs taken care of by supermarkets and health insurance, the goal for many of the brightest professionals became intellectual – to count, to matter, to fulfil childhood dreams. For these professionals, company life would prove too constraining and they found themselves migrating to Free Agent Nation.

Interestingly, many Free Agents soon found themselves employed by their old company! Both parties got what they wanted: the company only paid for the work done, and the Free Agent worked fewer hours for the same – if not much more – money.

Not just freelancers

A natural corollary of this behaviour was a brain drain. Corporations started to see their most valuable asset – the talent walk out of the building each night. To keep staff motivated – and in some cases to keep them at all – bosses had to start incentivizing their best members of staff differently.

When an employee came up with a good idea that the company just didn't have time for, the company knew that if they didn't support the idea there was every chance the employee would walk, taking their proposition, initiative and enthusiasm to the open market, to either a rival, or to become a rival.

When it comes to Free Agency, it's not what you do it's the way that you do it.

This saw the birth of the 'intrapreneur', people who build companies within companies, who work on special projects and at the cutting edge, sometimes for a slice of equity. These are as much Free Agents as the self-employed.

And these intrapreneurs behave like other Free Agents, only within an organization.

Another change that created the right atmosphere for the growth of Free Agency was access to capital. Many more people now have capital (or equity) in their homes which they can use to fund ventures or as security to get a loan. At the same time, the venture capital (VC) industry exploded and became more speculative about the entrepreneurs it would back. This followed Wall Street's junk bond bonanza of the eighties and nineties which backed riskier entrepreneurs but offered higher rates to their investors, and consequently took a lot of business away from the big VC funds. Now anyone with a good business plan was capable of attracting backers, even if they didn't go to the right university or work for the right City firm. It's not surprising that the number of new companies incorporated in the second half of the nineties was far greater than in the first half.

Moonlighting

While many Free Agents started new ventures at the expense of old ones, others simply grafted them on to their existing life. Once upon a time, doing a bit of work on the side was a sackable offence, but in Free Agent Nation it's likely to get you promoted!

Most employers will never be very happy if they find out that you have been doing a bit of freelance or consultancy work for a rival, but if your moonlighting is for an allied employer, they will probably be impressed. For instance, academics who write books on their subject tend to enhance the reputation of the institutions that employ them – and everyone's happy.

As we will see in later chapters, successful Free Agency has much to do with visibility and your ability to market yourself and your talent. So even though not all moonlighting involves earning money, it might well be worth doing. Some workers study at night school; others do voluntary work because they know the investments they make in themselves will be rewarded by their employer – whether that's their existing one or their next one! Workers who value themselves enough to put themselves through extra training or learning will see their value in the job market rise as their contemporaries stagnate. Some employers – relieved that any study is taking place out of office hours – will even make a financial contribution towards the costs of courses.

Freelancers, consultants, entrepreneurs and part-timers

As we have seen, the birth of Free Agent Nation has been a gradual process. Some have found their way there because they had no other choice – corporate asylum seekers, if you will – others were economic migrants who could see that the grass really was greener on the other side.

Free Agent Nation isn't just a home for freelancers and people who work alone sending in invoices to distant accounts departments who may lose track of payments. The most dynamic people in the workforce live in Free Agent Nation. You'll find them within organizations making money for themselves as well as their employer, in meetings with organizations as consultants or contributors, or in the park brainstorming with other Free Agents.

The land of the Free isn't a real place – it's a state of mind.

chapter three
the benefits of being a free agent

Feeling better already

There are some obvious benefits in becoming a Free Agent. For some it will involve ditching the commute (or at least not doing it five days a week), being able to take advantage of cheap mid-week travel offers, or going to your kid's sports day without losing annual leave. The list of clear measurable benefits is almost endless. But the first, immediate and *enduring* benefit is a little less tangible …

For most of our working lives we do what we are asked to do when we are asked to do it. We arrive at a location that's been decided by someone else at a time that's been been decided by someone else. We drink a brand of coffee that we haven't chosen and perform tasks to someone else's brief. For most people, the lack of responsibility for making such decisions is fine, but probably that's not you – otherwise you would have stopped reading by now. You may already have a hunch that once you adopt some of the basic tenets of Free Agency (listed in the Rules section of this book), something wonderful will start to happen.

When you work with a diary that only contains deadlines you yourself have set, that only involves doing work *you* want to do at a

price *you* have agreed to do it, and in the manner *you* choose to do it, then you be filled with an enormous sense of well-being.

When you are truly in control of your day and your destiny, you have more power and you walk a little taller.

When you combine with that the fact that no boss or client can dump work on your desk without your prior agreement, those feelings of resentment that can make work toxic simply disappear. No one can treat you like a doormat ever again. The sense of freedom won't take long to seep into every corner and crevice of your life and your psyche. Free Agency feels wonderful. It's a release.

Good for your pocket

One of the very best things about Free Agency is that – unlike almost anything else you can think of – on this occasion what's good for your soul is also good for your pocket! As we have touched on already, earning money from more than one source can protect you if one employer goes under, changes direction or simply has no need of your services any more. This basic fact has frustrated many Free Agents over the years who – when applying for a mortgage or a loan – find themselves less desirable than their more vulnerable counterparts on salary!

Freelancers and contractors generally take home more money than people doing the same work on staff. There are a number of reasons for this. First, by charging by the job, you can charge a premium for convenience. Second, you may also be able to sell the same piece of work a number of times over for the same amount of effort. Third, as you don't spend your time making unnecessary journeys or mithering about office politics, you will probably have more time to do more work and therefore earn more money.

Your day-to-day expenses will decrease too – you will no longer be paying for a commute you don't have to make, no longer paying for a Starbucks' latte when you can make one at home for a few pence. There'll be no more comfort shopping in your lunch hour to make up for a terrible day, because terrible days will be behind you once you make the leap.

If you add to that the benefits of taking care of your tax yourself, you increase your net income too. As a self-employed person, you can offset some of your living, travel and even clothing expenses against tax. The cost of computer equipment can be partially offset against the amount you finally owe the taxman. And as you pay your tax in a lump sum, it can be earning interest for you before you write out a cheque! On top of this you could also register for VAT. You have no legal obligation to do this if you earn less than £51,000 per annum, but if you can handle the extra paperwork it creates, it often means you're better off. To simplify: you charge VAT on all the work you do, but you get to claim VAT back on all the invoices you pay. So if you're going to be buying a lot of expensive computer hardware or other supplies, while earning a modest amount, you could well end up quids in!

But even if you are an intrapreneur or simply using Free Agency techniques to improve your working relationships at your existing job, you too will be better off financially. In times of recession or trouble, your company is going to hold on to someone as bright and committed as you, long after your plodding colleagues have been handed their P45s. And even in good times, you're more likely to get promoted, get a pay rise or a bonus if you behave like a Free Agent.

Your own boss

Even if you work for a nice guy whom you respect, from time to time you're going to go home bitching about him. It doesn't matter who your boss is or how fantastic they are, none of us really likes being told what to do. Now imagine that – by negotiating Free Agent working conditions – you are an equal with any employer. How would that change your day? Suddenly they need you as much as you need them. Which means that they have to treat you with the same respect you show them. If you are a contractor or freelancer you set your own deadlines (obviously in consultation with your client). You decide if you would rather work through the night so you can have a long weekend somewhere lovely. That's the kind of tough decision making you're going to have to get used to now you're the boss.

Not only does Free Agency change your relationship with your boss, it changes your relationship with your co-workers. When you are furthering your own agenda – i.e. your Free Agent career – by carrying out a piece of work, you don't have to worry about anyone else's agenda. You can leave tedious and toxic bitching and point-scoring behind you.

And as your own boss, you can choose what kind of work you do. You can balance work you really, really want to do that maybe doesn't pay that well, with other work that pays better. By working on a variety of projects you will be more stimulated and find reward from several sources. Your day may now involve several different elements rather than an endless trudge at someone else's bidding. Your boss can no longer cherry-pick the best bits. You might have to do a bit more of the dross, but you are also guaranteed the cream. Being a portfolio worker creates variety, and if the cliché's true, then you'd better get used to the taste of spice.

More time

Through better time management and earning more per hour than you did previously, *and* by working more efficiently, you can – if you choose – work fewer hours. This may help you take care of your family commitments or it may just help you get to the gym before the 6 pm rush.

What it should also do is give you the time to do your work better. That might mean actually reading the relevant trade publication that would make you better informed, or attending conferences and debates associated with your work. Just a few hours extra a week might be enough to learn a new skill that will increase the services you can offer to clients and also the services you can charge for. And the chances are that the better you are at doing something, the more you will enjoy doing it.

Me plc is like any other business – if you don't evolve you die.

You may simply have more time to think. No business can move forward without fresh ideas.

This thinking time will open your mind to new opportunities, opportunities you would otherwise miss if you were too busy chasing someone else's tail for them. Quite simply, Free Agents live a richer life.

Don't wait for retirement

As mentioned earlier, the chances of today's workers retiring at age 60 or 65 are slim. So if you're planning on waiting until some magical time in the future to move to Provence, play golf or buy a classic Jag, you could be waiting for a very, very long time. Free Agency is about incorporating your retirement into your working life.

If you enjoy your life as a Free Agent, the chances are you won't stop – even when you get to 100. Free Agency isn't just about taking a holistic approach to your working day, but to your working life. It's enjoying life today, not putting dreams on hold for a future that may never arrive.

So if it's important to you to protest about global pollution – go out and do it. If starting your day with a jog will help you cope with your work – put your running shoes on. If being able to help your kids with their homework would make their school lives happier – just put it in your diary.

You are now in control. Not your boss, or your company, or your pension provider. You. You set your own priorities and go for them.

Now, doesn't that feel good?

Major benefits and drawbacks of being a Free Agent

Benefits	Drawbacks
More freedom	Need for self-discipline
More control over your work schedule	Total responsibility for project
Take as many days holiday as you like	No paid holidays
If you feel under the weather, you don't need to go into the office	No paid sick days
You're your own boss	No one else to blame when things go wrong
Self-esteem from doing your own thing	Sometimes working in isolation; need for self-motivation
You can grow your own company	You need to deal with the paperwork, tax, etc.
Potential for greater financial reward	May be troughs as well as peaks
Keeping yourself well trained in latest techniques and skillset to keep ahead of your rivals	You'll have to fund your own training and take time out to attend
Variety in roles you'll have to perform (sales, publicity, finance, admin, IT support)	May need training in some aspects. Need to manage your time effectively
Work from home	Temptation to just keep working
Tax-deductible expenses	You have to sort out your own tax return or get an accountant to do it

chapter four
the problems of being a free agent

What's the catch?

Anything that's as liberating, empowering and fun as Free Agency usually comes with a catch. Usually it's money. And to be fair, with Free Agency, money is a major reason why more people don't take the plunge.

Leaving a regular, reliable source of income behind requires forward planning. If you were to leave your job tomorrow, how long would it take you to find work? And then once you've done the work, how long will it take for your invoices to be paid?

Ah yes, invoices. Free Agency sounds like a nightmare of paperwork and chasing accounts departments for overdue cheques. What if you're not very good at paperwork, or have as much idea of what your bank balance is as you do about the national debt of Bolivia? If you've no experience of taking responsibility for your finances and have always lived blissfully in the knowledge that more money just arrives in your account each month, you could be in for a shock. There is no shirking from the fact that you are going to have to get to grips with your paperwork. It doesn't have to be hard – you just open up a spreadsheet and keep a track of your income and your outgoings. There is more advice on this later in the book, but rest assured that it's not difficult and there are plenty of simple software packages that can do most of the work for you.

The truth is that unless you have at least enough money to live for two months before you expect your first cheque to arrive, you're going to find yourself short. Even that might not be enough if your first cheque is just for a few hundred pounds. It's no wonder then that many Free Agents start by moonlighting and don't make the break until they have enough work coming in. Others are simply enabled to take the Free Agency plunge after receiving a redundancy package. Or some just have to save up for while until they have a big enough financial cushion. But even if these options aren't available to you, you will find other sources of contingency finance in the final chapter, Money Management. The point is that – as with most things in life – where there's a will there's a way.

Annual leave – a thing of the past

In your calculations you also have to allow for the fact that – if you leave full-time employment – you will no longer get such benefits as holiday pay, parental leave or sick pay. Recently introduced employment law states that if you work for a company continually for 13 weeks – as a freelancer or contractor – you are entitled by law to have a week's paid leave. If you work part time this is pro rata.

While it's the law, many employers aren't aware of it yet and some will tell you to take a running jump when you invoice for days you weren't even in the country. You have to judge for yourself what you need more – the paid leave or the next contract. The tips in the chapter on Negotiation should help.

Sick pay is a different matter. Many people who phone in sick aren't actually that sick. They are just not up to the commute, the bitching and whatever else their day involves on top of the work. Most of them would be capable of working in their dressing gowns at the kitchen table. You have to accept now that – if deadlines of clients demand – you will have to work through minor bouts of colds or flu. Because if you take a day off sick, you might be losing more than a day's money.

As a Free Agent you might want to think now about certain back-up plans. Maybe you could subcontract the work? Maybe you could get help with domestic chores to free up your remaining strength to focus on the work?

You also need to think about the worst-case scenarios. What if you were seriously ill and couldn't work for months or years? How would you cope financially? It may be appropriate to think about some kind of insurance, both for health cover and for loss of income.

Paperwork

The other aspect of paperwork that sometimes deters potential free agents is the tax return. How many of us have shuddered when the buff envelope stamped 'Inland Revenue' lands on the doormat? Just about all of us.

Every worker in Britain now has to fill in a self-assessment tax return. If you've been PAYE all your life this may come as a bit of a shock. But there really is nothing to fear if you have kept track of your earnings and expenses.

Like most of the administrative tasks of running a business – and that's what Me plc is – filling in your tax return can easily be outsourced. An accountant will charge you a few hundred pounds and will hope to save that money on your final tax bill by exploiting their knowledge of tax law to the full.

But as the first rule of Free Agency is responsibility, why not make the decision to take care of your tax return yourself? The Tax Office really does make it easy for you and can calculate for you the tax you have to pay. You can even complete your return online. And if you do your tax return yourself, it's one less person to chase, one less bill to pay, and you can rest easy knowing that it's been taken care of.

Computers

The chances of you being a Free Agent who doesn't use a computer are next to zero.

Just as you've got to learn to love your tax return, you'll have to get intimately acquainted with your Mac or PC.

Now that you don't have an IT department to call or a central server storing all your key files, you'll have to learn to take care of those things yourself.

The first rule is simple: *back up*. Imagine you lost a project you had been working on for a client for a month. You can't charge for what you don't deliver and there's no one else who's quickly going to piece the work together again for you.

Nor can you afford to clog up your phone line holding on to an IT helpline for hours. You could well miss a vital offer. You certainly can't afford for your computer – essentially your office – to be taken away and mended for a few days. If you're computer-phobic, getting to grips with this will be a real problem, but you have no choice. If you need to go to night school to learn PC maintenance or you need to pay extra insurance that ensures data recovery and immediate replacement, then this is simply something you have to swallow.

It's essential to install a virus checker or firewall software to protect you from accidentally importing, and unknowingly spreading, any 'bugs'. These can arrive via email and can look quite innocuous, until you open them! Some viruses and worms can even destroy your hard disk. Every so often you'll need to update the software (normally via the supplier's website).

To reassure you, most problems can be avoided by using your computer in the right way in the first place (i.e. not spilling your tea on the keyboard), by running regular 'disk doctor' programs and by learning a few tricks. Don't be scared, just do it.

Where do you find work?

Sadly, there isn't a map that can point you in the right direction. But you can be sure of one thing – you have to go out and find work.

Don't wait for work to find you, or you're in for a very long stretch on Skint Street.

No wonder then that, for many, it's this first hurdle that is the biggest problem.

The techniques you'll learn later on in the book will help with your search for work, but you should start thinking now about companies you would approach for work. If yours is a skill that can be exploited by a recruitment or temp agency, it's worth talking to them now about your skills and availability. But the thing that will really bring you work will be personal recommendation. If you do a good first job for a client, they will book you for a second. And then they will recommend you to others. And so it will go on.

So before you embark on a Free Agency career, you will have to make sure that your skills are marketable and that there is a big enough market for you to sell your services to. By the time you've finished this book, you'll have all the skills you need in order to be confident – you won't be worrying about finding work any more.

Loneliness

While many Free Agents cite office politics as a major reason for flying the corporate nest, some still miss the buzz of an office. There's no one to bounce ideas off, grab a coffee with or talk to about last night's TV.

The truth is though, that most Free Agents aren't sitting at their desk in an isolated farmhouse far from human company. They're in meetings, on courses, networking or on temporary contracts in offices with other Free Agents. You may have to become more disciplined about arranging to meet friends, co-workers and clients, but a successful Free Agent is never lonely.

chapter five
are you a free agent?

Ready for responsibility

If you have ever said to yourself, your co-workers or your boss that you 'want more responsibility', then it's quite likely that Free Agency is for you. If you feel you can do more than your current position within a company will allow, then you have the makings of a fine Free Agent. If you currently use less than the full complement of strings on your bow and this frustrates you, then you should definitely be considering Free Agency. A Free Agent uses all their wits, wiles and skills to get satisfied.

Free Agency often suits confident people who get personal reward from self-expression. But it also requires sensitivity and people skills as you are going to work with a wider variety of co-workers and clients. There's no point being 'the big I am' when your colleague on one project could well be your boss on the next. Rather than being confident in yourself, you must be confident in your ability.

Keep motivated – Free Agents can't afford to be lazy.

You certainly need to be smart and you need to be disciplined – especially when it comes to quality thresholds, deadlines, paperwork and money.

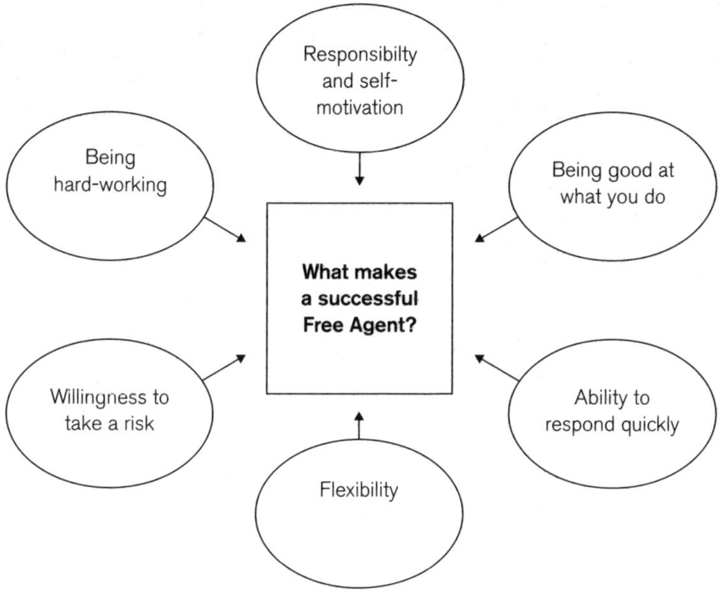

It will also help if you're naturally positive, otherwise a couple of refusals or unanswered phone calls could send you into a morose tailspin of despair.

Of course, there isn't just one personality type that makes a good Free Agent, the only absolute rule is that you must be adult enough to take the responsibility.

Knowledge is power

The one characteristic that almost all successful Free Agents share is that they are mature, i.e. they are not green school-leavers. This is because what you are selling as a Free Agent is your knowledge, your experience, your contacts and your track record. Some Free Agents are recent graduates or school-leavers, but selling yourself on enthusiasm and energy only gets you so far.

The management writer Charles Handy has mapped out what he believes is the likely career path of most Free Agents. They will spend the first ten years of their careers working for big organizations – what he calls elephants – soaking up training, qualifications, contacts, specialist knowledge and the personal skills that allow them to operate efficiently in the business world.

After this, he argues, the brightest and the best will become frustrated and deluded with corporate life and leave to become Free Agents – what he calls fleas – often selling their services back to the company they've just left.

This is of course a simplification, but it contains a basic truth about Free Agency – you have to have something real to offer. No matter how much responsibility you want, how outgoing you are or how good you are at time management, if you haven't got something to sell then there's no point going to market. To take this one stage further, you're still not going to cut the mustard as a Free Agent unless someone is going to buy your skills at that market.

This is where the rise in corporate literacy has helped so many people make the move to Free Agent Nation. Their basic understanding of market forces has taught them that not only do they have to have something to sell, they have to be able to sell it *and* be able to find customers. This basic law of profit lies behind all successful Free Agency.

As a Free Agent you will probably find yourself with competition. Even if you are the only person on the planet who knows about your specialist area, you will be in competition with all the other demands being made on the person with whom you have a contract.

No matter what you do, you have to have a unique selling proposition.

This may be the fact that you are undeniably the best in your field, or that you combine two different skillsets. It may be specialist knowledge or any number of individual factors, but you should remember that it's just as likely to be that you have a reputation for sticking to the brief and delivering on time. Often the most valuable commodity you are selling is convenience.

So assuming that you have the desire to be Free and the talent to make it, what else do you need?

Know your strengths

This is the key to making it on your own. Before you decide whether or not you are going to have a happy and fulfilled life as a Free Agent, you must first get to know yourself.

This isn't easy as we often make the mistake of thinking we already know ourselves. In truth, few of us do, as our egos protect us from the awful truth. Just as the guy in the office with a body odour problem is the last person to notice the smell, none of us is very good at acknowledging our weaknesses.

If you're hoping to make a career as a graphic designer, for example, you need to find out how good a graphic designer you really are. Do you have any awards to prove your talent, or have you ever had serious praise from a boss or client that you could use as a reference? And even if you're good at what you're designing now, you have to ask yourself if you are capable of taking on more complex or bigger projects? Are you capable of mastering several styles?

If you are honest – really honest – with yourself (and it may well be worth asking trusted friends and colleagues for their opinion about your merits), you may find that, sadly, you're not quite as brilliant as you first thought. But this may actually be a good thing.

By carefully assessing your skillset you may discover that your best or most marketable skill is that you are fast, or easy-going, or available to work nights, or make a great pot of tea or have specialist knowledge of Oriental art history. Any of these things could, for the right client, in combination with basic competence in your field, make you more employable than the best graphic designer in the world.

List your assets

Your strengths might surprise you. A good way of finding out exactly where your strengths lie is to get a big sheet of paper and make several lists. Your lists should have the following headings: Skills, Attributes, Knowledge, Dreams, People and Money. Under Skills, list everything you can demonstrate you are good at. It might be related to your work; it might not be.

Under Attributes, include everything else you offer. That may be attention to detail, it could be that you relish a challenge. Under Knowledge, write down everything you know about. Again this might not relate to your profession, it may include things as diverse and apparently useless as Tottenham Hotspur strikers from 1980–2001, or the chronology of the pharaohs.

Your Dreams column should include everything you want to achieve in your life from a season ticket to the opera, to children, to travel, to being a millionaire. Just put it all down.

Now, under the People heading, make a list of *everyone* you know. Not just your mates, family and colleagues – think of friends of friends, past colleagues, the guy who fixes your car or your kids' teachers. Absolutely everyone. In the Money column, make a list of your traditional assets – your finances. How much equity have you got in your flat? How big is your student loan? What's in your piggy bank? Taking our wannabe designer as an example, the table shows how an asset list shapes up (clearly, this is not very extensive and just to give you an idea).

Skills	**Attributes**	**Knowledge**	**Dreams**	**People**	**Money**
Photoshop	Methodical	Tudor history	House by the sea	Other designers	£1,000 savings
Quark	Flexible	Seattle music	Paint	Jim in the army	£300 credit card
Illustrator	Punctual	Brit art	MG Roadster	Gallery owners	Good credit with the bank
Mac and PC	Relaxed			Musicians	
Guitar				Pete behind the bar	
Cooking				Clara the photographer	

It's worth taking your time with your asset list. Leave it lying around and come back to it from time to time – let it build into a true and complete portraint of your life.

As you compile it you may notice themes develop and just studying may reveal what your Free Agent assets are. However, it might not be that clear, so photocopy it several times and arm yourself with some coloured pens. Colour code the most important assets, see if you can work out the following:

- The most important thing you can offer.
- The most valuable reward you can get.

This will help you negotiate with clients.

But before you use that information, you need to find those clients. So, taking a fresh photocopy, use the pens to forge connections between different entries on your list. Whether you can put contacts in touch with each other, or offer a skill in conjunction with a contact, every connection you make increases the worth on your asset list.

Your assets increase in value the moment you realise what you can do with them. Now, taking the example of the designer, it appears, would be happier working on projects relating to art or music, but in these flaky professions it might be her attributes that make her more employable than her software knowledge. Certainly, her love of these areas is more likely to lead to work over her knowledge of the Tudors. Given that her dreams are relatively modest (she's not wanting to be the next Tracey Emin or drive a Lotus Elise), she might be happier working part time to focus on her painting and music.

Looking at her People column, some of her contacts seem to have a lot in common. Jim doesn't look like he'd be much help in the hunt for work, but many of the others will know people who know people. She needs to start seeing herself at the centre of web with ever-extending contacts that will lead to money. Another way to make money out of her contacts would be to put them in touch with each other – working as a collective of Free Agents might be lucrative as well as fun. It certainly looks like she's got more chance landing work through word of mouth than through the classifieds. She needs to start making her contacts work harder for her. Perhaps somewhere in her address book is someone she can work with, sell to, or subcontract work out to.

Contacts are the most valuable currency in Free Agent Nation.

Finally, the Money column is fine, but if she were to rely on freelance income alone, she would probably need to build up a bigger cash reserve first. What this should tell her is that she can't afford to take on risky work that might take too long to pay, if it pays at all. Another person's asset list may display that their fabulous wealth is their most interesting asset – in which case risk can be embraced.

Play to your strengths

The point of finding out where your strengths lie, whatever they may be, is to make sure that you exploit them correctly. A big part of making yourself a Free Agent will be your ability to work out what people will pay you to do. You may not be able to make your knowledge of Manchester United pay (and therefore your season ticket tax-deductible!) but you may be able to impress your employer with your bulging contacts book or your ability to deliver a finished job days before anyone else. Your most valuable skill is quite likely to be something that doesn't come with a certificate. If you think laterally, new options will materialize and more doors will open. If this seems like a more sensible way of conducting business to you, then you're already on the bus to Free Agent Nation.

01

part one
the rules

In this section of the book you will learn the eight rules of Free Agency. You will learn why they are important and how to incorporate them into your working day. A Free Agent who lives by the Rules and uses the Tools (covered in the next section) will maximize their chances of finding work, earning more money and getting satisfaction.

rule one
be responsible

No one else is to blame

All the rules of Free Agency are important, but this one underwrites them all. Along with the rights to set your own timetable, to choose your own work, to take today off because the sun is shining, comes the responsibility of taking care of yourself, your co-workers and your clients.

As discussed in the first part of this book, one of the scariest things about Free Agency is losing the right to blame other people for the fact you are not where you want to be. Throughout our lives we blame our upbringing, the postman or the bus driver for letting us down. As a Free Agent, only you can let yourself down. If your systems or your suppliers let you down, it's your fault for relying on an infrastructure that you don't control. You can read this two ways:

- Shit happens, and there's nothing you can do about it.
- Shit happens, and therefore you always need a back-up plan or a safety-net.

Either way, as the buck now stops with you, you no longer pass it down the line. You deal with it.

One of the fundamentals of Free Agency is that we start to interact with each other as equals: you want the work as much as the guy handing out the contract wants the work done. This is the basic principle of all your Free Agent negotiations. And as an equal, you have an equal responsibility to bring plans to fruition.

Obviously you might not really, *really* want to do some of the work you contract to do (you may see it as a stepping stone, a favour or a financial necessity). However, once you have agreed to do it, or have signed to do it, you stop your whinging, your bitching and your procrastinating right there and then. As every bit of work you do as a Free Agent will be done on terms you yourself will have negotiated, you have no excuse for not sticking to the terms you agreed. If you're worried about the materials, the people or the conditions you will be working with, this is something you negotiate before you sign a contract (or agree to do the work). If you don't like the conditions, the people etc., then don't sign. Because once the ink is dry, you can only blame yourself if parts don't arrive on time, subcontractors let you down or computers crash.

You're in control; you take the responsibility.

As a professional, you should know how long a job will take, how hard it will be and what it will involve. You also know at what price you are prepared to take the job on. So if you sign a contract that ends up biting you on the arse because you didn't think it through, then it's your fault. Not the guy who (you now tell everyone) forced you to sign it at gun-point.

Learn from everything and everyone

Similarly, if you start a new job happy with the salary you negotiated but two weeks later find that the girl at the next desk – who does exactly the same job as you – earns more money, you cannot moan and bitch about this fact. It's your fault. You should have done your homework and negotiated a better deal. One habit that will stand your Free Agent career in good stead will be your ability to learn from everything and everyone. Next time you will do your research better and negotiate a better contract. Or you will use it in some other way to your advantage in future negotiations.

Likewise, you can no longer blame the boss when your partner complains that you never go out any more or don't come home till you're too tired to do anything but sleep. It's your fault for not organizing your diary better, or managing your partner's expectations better. If you knew you'd be working so hard you wouldn't have time for fun for the past month, you should have communicated that better. Are you getting the picture?

Being the boss comes with added responsibilities – any manager will tell you that. Now that you are your own boss, you had better be ready to handle the obligations that come with your job title.

As your name is now attached to everything you do – you are no longer a faceless worker who can coast on others' achievements – one of the first responsibilities to yourself is always to be the best that you can be. You are as good as your last piece of work in many people's eyes, so your talent must not lapse. You owe it to yourself.

Know your place

As well as being responsible for yourself, you also carry responsibility for your role within an organization or project. If, for example, you are preparing some figures for an annual report and you deliver them late, you are letting down the printer who is waiting to print the report, the manager who needs the figures to determine how to move forward, and the board whose time you've wasted by not allowing them to act on the latest information.

Being a Free Agent is not about being the star of the show, it's about being the star of *your* show.

You are almost certainly just one of many cogs that turns the machinery of your company or industry. And as no cog can work without the others, you are as important as any other cog but no more so. If you are more efficient, the company can be more efficient as a whole. And everyone benefits. But if you louse up, the ramifications could hurt everyone.

Your responsibilities don't stop there either. As well as your duties to honour your contracts with grace, keep your loved ones happy, and never to let yourself down, you must also consider all the other responsibilities you have. Like making sure there's enough money in the bank to pay the rent, or completing your tax return by the correct deadline.

Essentially, being a Free Agent is about being a grown-up. You get to stay up late, choose to do fun work, take long holidays and plenty of other benefits, but only because you take care of your fundamental responsibilities to yourself and those around you.

rule two
be good

Got to be good

As a Free Agent, the main way you will attract business is almost certainly going to be word of mouth. Clever marketing and the gift of the gab will only get you so far. There's only one way to guarantee success – and that's by being good at what you do. Very good. This is written in stone in the constitution of Free Agent Nation.

Now that you are no longer guaranteed work for the indefinite future, you need to ensure that every piece of work you do will lead to another. If you get your first contract via a slick presentation, that doesn't mean you'll get the next gig automatically – you will only get it if your work is good enough. Just imagine, the company that's just used your services is asked to recommend you and they say, 'Well, the pitch was fantastic but we were disappointed in the end.' Disappointing an existing client is worse than coming a close second in the first place – now you'll never get another chance.

Given that it's far easier to retain existing contracts than win new ones, even if your clients never recommend you to anyone else, you will still need to keep your existing clients' business. Especially because once they trust you, you can start charging more: paying you a bit extra costs less than searching round for your untried replacement. Clearly then, one of the best ways of taking care of your clients is to take care of yourself.

Invest in yourself

If you are selling yourself as an accountant, then you need to be the best accountant you can be. If you are selling your skills in computer programming, then you cannot let those skills get rusty. Training is free if your employer has ever sent you on a course, it might have just seemed like a day out of the office: there wasn't much point in paying attention because the new skill wasn't going to get you a pay rise. The bad news is that you may no longer have an employer paying for your training, but the good news is that the cost of that training is now a tax-deductible expense – and it will help you earn more money.

No Free Agent can afford to be anything other than brilliant.

This means that when the new version of essential software comes out, you *have* to buy the upgrade and learn it. This means if a new qualification becomes the industry standard that you can't get hired without, then you *have* to get it. You must always keep your skills up to date. If there's something you haven't done for a while, then take a refresher course.

Producing good work also means delivering it complete and on time. It's about good communication with your co-workers and your colleagues. It's about being good to work with. So 'being good' starts when you negotiate how a certain piece of work is to be carried out; never agree to do anything without enough skills, resources or help to get you to the deadline in shape and on time. If you miss deadlines or produce incomplete work, you look bad. It's almost always within your (negotiating) power to make sure that you always look good – if you lay the right foundations.

Of course, as a Free Agent it's not just your skills you are selling – it's your knowledge and your contacts. You can't be good without them.

So if there is a trade publication for your industry, subscribe now. If a national newspaper carries a weekly supplement about your profession, tell your newsagent to keep you a copy. Not only is this a simple way of keeping abreast of industry developments, it's a good way to keep a check on what your contacts are doing. You should also read any relevant books that are published, reports issued by governing bodies, or visit relevant exhibitions and events.

If you work from home a lot, it's especially important that you maintain your contacts. Make the effort to attend industry events. Arrange lunch or use email to keep in touch with people whose opinions you value, whose company you enjoy, and who have knowledge and/or contacts you will want to exploit in the future. This may lead directly to work, but more likely it will just keep your knowledge up to date, allow you to take a temperature reading on any hot issues, or allow you to see other sides of industry arguments. It also means your name is in people's minds when they're asked if they know someone who can do the things you do.

Do unto others ...

Now we move on to the other definition of being good. Just because you don't work with the same people every day, just because you don't have a boss to suck up to, just because you're off for a mid-week break – that doesn't mean you can start to treat co-workers how you like. Far from it.

A good saying to remember is that, in Free Agent Nation, what goes around comes around. Free Agency works because of trust. You do a piece of work on the trust that the cheque will come. You get given the contract on the trust that you will do the work.

Money doesn't make the Free Agent world go round – trust does!

When you are relying on your contacts to bring you work, you owe it to yourself to be thoroughly decent in your dealings with them. So as well as sticking to any contractual obligations you may have with them, you also want to be nice to them. It's always worth doing someone a favour, because one day they may be in a position to return the favour to you. If Free Agency is your new religion then this is one of its solemn commandments: Do Unto Others as You Would Have Done Unto You.

If you're going to make a success of being a Free Agent, you'll soon learn that it's not about making a fast buck and running as fast as you can from the scene of your crime. It's about doing the best you can do and being the best you can be. This, your guru will tell you, is your path to fulfilment and happiness. Free Agent Nation is the Promised Land!

And if you want to get really noble about it, it's also about the Greater Good. You might make a personal sacrifice now for a chance of a reward or payback many years hence, either because your favour will be returned or your investment will pay dividends. It's about doing work you believe in with people you trust. That feels good, doesn't it?

rule three
be visible

Get noticed to get on

If you don't get noticed, you won't get on. It's as simple as that. If no one knows who you are, how are they going to reward you? If no one knows you exist, how are they going to hire you? Whether you are an employee or a freelancer, the single biggest differentiator in your career will be your ability to get noticed.

In business, as in everything else, people like to hook their cart to a winning pony. They like to buy brands they trust. They like to brag about smart moves they've made, winners they've backed. Successful Free Agency involves selling yourself as a product – a smart, dynamic product that makes people feel good just for buying you.

The Free Agent challenge is to make yourself as attractive as Coca-Cola.

It's all about marketing. Even though it's claimed that most people prefer Pepsi in blind taste tests, Coca-Cola is the world's leading soft drink brand. And that's all down to marketing.

The tools you'll learn in this chapter will enable you to get a profile, get recognized for the work you do, and get ahead.

Let's start by considering what makes people a 'famous' brand at work. Usually it's because of the work they have done – their professional achievements – either in their current role or a previous one. You may recognize them when you enter the office for the first time because you've read about them in trade newspapers.

Another kind of office fame comes from simply staying on one place for a long time – you become associated with the company and everyone within that company knows where to find you, just like they know where the photocopier is.

Some people build up their profile at the Christmas party by pouring beer over the boss's husband or by pretending to be one of the Kids From Fame on the dancefloor.

Others get a kind of reflected fame. The 'she worked with Elton John/the chief exec on Project Such-And-Such' type of fame.

It's pretty obvious from this rundown which are the best ways to make a name for yourself: by doing good work and associating with the best people. You don't want to get a reputation as a berk who can't handle their liquor. You certainly don't want to become the kind of legend that gets overlooked along with the pot plants when exciting work is being handed out. It should be fairly clear by now that – if you're not doing it already – you should be starting to build your corporate profile. But how do you do it?

Brand You

The American management 'guru' (this seems to be his official title as he is never referred to as anything else!) Tom Peters has written much about 'Brand You' and a lot of his work is relevant to Free Agents.

To brand yourself, start to think about your most saleable attributes. As you work on branding, consider not only what you are already best known for, but also the things you'd rather be known for.

Consider the image you want to project, what Brand You stands for, and what your personal brand's values are.

Let's start by thinking about how existing supermarket brands attract our business. All supermarkets offer the same mix of goods – food, cleaning products and toothpaste – yet they offer completely different services. Marks & Spencer's food hall is the sort of place you go to buy treats – ready meals and fancy bread, or cheese and port selections for Christmas presents. At the other end of the scale, Lidl is the place to head for bulk buys of pet food and toilet paper. Marks & Spencer has its shops in affluent areas, while Lidl operates in poorer neighbourhoods.

Both businesses are sound and profitable, and although one might seem more desirable from a consumer's point of view, from an investor's point of view it's Lidl that's seen the boom in recent years. The lesson here is that you can brand yourself in a number of different ways to maximize your Free Agent potential. A good brand isn't necessarily a 'posh' brand – it's one that accurately conveys the business behind the logo.

Your brand values are characteristics that can either limit or propel your career. For instance, let's take a look at the Virgin brand. If Richard Branson's original record company's brand had been about music, he would not be Britain's best-known entrepreneur.

The Virgin Group's success lies in the fact that its brand values transcend each industry in which it operates.

Virgin brand values are about taking on the big boys and doing it better; about bringing panache and passion to tired industries.

Branson has done this time and time again with airlines, mobile phones and financial services. His personal values of taking on the establishment while having a bit of fun form the bedrock of Virgin's growth, not the bands he originally signed to his music label. So now you see why choosing and marketing the right brand values can have a significant effect on your earning potential.

Choosing your brand values

As we saw with M&S and Lidl, it's not enough to decide just to be a cleaner – you must decide what *sort* of cleaner you want to be. You could run a cleaning business where you turn up some time between Monday and Sunday for a couple of hours light housework before taking the cash that's been left for you under the phone. Or you might turn up in a uniform with a name badge at 9 am every Tuesday and send an invoice once a month. Both are fine, but one style of operation naturally lends itself to different sorts of clients, different sorts of jobs and probably also different rates of pay.

Your brand values – and your marketing in general – have to dovetail exactly with your personal and professional ambitions for Free Agency. If your only ambition is to make as much money as possible, then cultivate an image that is going to attract the biggest number of high-paying clients. If, however, you want to use your talents to secure world peace, then your brand values are going to have to convey something different altogether!

Keep in mind that your brand is something you're selling – it therefore has to be desirable to a large number of people. Your brand identity probably won't contain certain aspects of your personality or lifestyle that mean a lot to you (like your love of angling or fondness for rubber underwear) but which won't help you find work. Your brand identity will be about your professionalism, your flair, enthusiasm, commitment or other positive attributes.

Imagine: you have the choice to hire one of two architects. One presents himself as positive, amenable, capable, trustworthy and prudent. The other has more flair and you like her designs more, but she seems flaky, scatty and uncompromising about some alterations you wanted to make. You have a clear choice – you can hire the 'mad-but-brilliant' branded architect, or the 'reliable-and-capable' branded architect . Your choice will depend on the work you want done, but these professionals' self-branding are what will help you make that choice.

So you can be a lawyer. Or you can be the lawyer that wins cases. Or the lawyer who does his own paperwork. Or the lawyer that will take on *pro bono* work that no one else will. Or the lawyer whose sharp suits and sophisticated manner attracts a better class of client. Get it?

Working on Brand You may take a long time, and your brand may evolve as you mature and acquire new skills. But thinking about the image you portray in the short term will help you achieve your long-term goals.

Ten ways to get noticed in the office

Once you have decided on the best face to show the world, you'll need some sure-fire tips to make sure your brand recognition rate is higher than your rival's:

Be friendly

Don't you hate sitting just a few feet away from someone who's clearly a new member of staff, but you have no idea who they are? So does everyone else. So if you're new, make a point of introducing yourself to the people who work near you and tell them what you've been hired to do. Ask them their names and what they do for the organization. And if you go to conferences, wear a name badge – not only will this help people know your name, it will help them remember it.

Dress the part

This is obvious, but if you work in an office where everyone wears suits, wear a suit yourself. The rule is to dress appropriately for the situation. But if it's a casual office, don't be tempted to go to work in your jogging bottoms or pyjamas: wear clean, new smart-but-casual clothes. If you're meeting a client for a drink after work, change your accessories. Keep your hair the way your hairdresser means it to be. Don't wear overpowering perfume or aftershave. As your grandmother would say: keep yourself nice. And don't be tempted to inject a little personality into your office persona with a Simpsons tie or Barbie headband. Whatever your brand – this is *always* off brand!

Produce good work

At the heart of every successful Free Agent is a good worker. If you're sloppy, late or wrong your brand will suffer – a brand that doesn't deliver on its promise is a dud. You have to be Good to be Free. Eventually people will notice. You might not get an immediate return, but your brand will have longevity as people you worked with years ago will continue to recommend you for new contracts.

Go to the pub

When your boss, colleague or client suggests a drink at lunch or after work, say yes. It's a chance for you to get to know your client, your colleague or your company better (and maybe learn something or meet someone that could benefit you greatly), but it's also a chance for them to get to know you for something other than the job in hand. Discuss other projects, other skills and other successes. NB don't get drunk; don't just talk about yourself – you should find out if they could be a useful contact; do buy a round; and make sure you show your best side.

Give good presentations

Bosses and clients may never remember you from one of hundreds of employees or potential contractors. So if you get the chance to present to your board or to a new client – either by pitching for business or just to go over the quarterly review – make this time count. Be a star. This is your chance to highlight your personal abilities and successes so you have to learn to give good presentations (see the chapter on Pitching). Likewise, make sure your name is on the cover of any report you write or document you send out. Get your name under people's noses as often as possible.

Coverage in newsletters

If you've won an award, a contract or a competition – tell your company newsletter or trade publication. If there's a photo of you shaking some bigwig's hand or standing behind a celebrity at a launch of a new detergent, send that in too. Don't be shy – speak to anyone who's ever worked for a company newsletter or trade rag and they'll tell you that they need to get sent this kind of stuff. If you have a marketing department, tell them of your success. The trick here is that if people have heard of you, they will assume you are good, well connected and an industry star.

Take on extra work

This is one sure way to get noticed! Whether it's for a client, your company or a charitable use of your time, just doing more work brings you into contact with more people, which in turn gets your name better known. And for the right reasons too.

Watch *EastEnders* and the World Cup!

Or indulge in any other pastime that allows you to talk to colleagues and engage them in something other than work. You might sit near people you don't have to talk to for work, but if they get to know you through office chitchat this may open many doors for your career.

Win awards

This leads us being back to being good at what you do. If you're good and you can tell people about it, you will be a very successful Free Agent. So nominate yourself for competitions, or arrange with a mate to always nominate each other.

Work late/early

If you work in an office – especially an open-plan office – with other people, an easy way for people to get to know you for the right reasons is to regularly be seen in the office at the beginning or end of the day. You might be in at 8 am because you want to avoid the worst of the rush hour, or still around at 8 pm because you're meeting friends or took a long lunch, but it's a good chance to get to know the people in your organization who really do the work that counts. If this isn't your boss, it will be the movers and shakers who are working on secret projects, or the person planning to be the next boss.

Professional indemnity insurance/public liability insurance

Depending on the type of business/services you'll be offering, it may be worth taking out (a) public liability insurance to protect yourself against being sued by a member of the public (e.g. if they have an accident while on your premises) and (b) professional indemnity insurance to protect your firm or yourself from being sued by another company for misleading advice or unprofessional behaviour (e.g. if they lost a contract because you failed to deliver by the agreed deadline and/or to the required standard). This is not something to worry most Free Agents, but something to consider as your business grows.

Business name registration

Another way to get noticed is to give your company a memorable or imposing name. If you're a sole trader or a small firm that has decided not to register as a limited company, you can still protect your firm's identity by registering your business name. Business Names Registration will do a search to check if the name you intend to use has been registered to another user. If it has, you'll have to choose a different name. If you don't do your homework and start calling your firm a name that has already been registered in the same market sector, you could open yourself up to litigation. For an annual fee of around £50 you can register and protect your company name.

Registering a domain name

Once a Free Agent has set up in business, it is vital even before the name of the company is decided, to ensure that you get hold of the domain name you want. You'll need it for email addresses and websites; even if you don't intend using these straight away. Someone else may have already registered it, so get in as early as you can! Anyone can register a domain name, it doesn't cost much money and there have been cases of individuals 'hijacking' names of famous companies and asking exorbitant amounts of money to resell the domain name back to the original company. Even if you just want to register using your own name (John.Smith.com), you'll probably find it's already been registered (maybe not actively used) and then you'll need to come up with a different name or variation. So securing the domain name should go hand-in-hand with deciding what you'll be calling your business (for invoices, etc.). You may decide to register the business name and the domain name simultaneously. You have to pay separately for .com and .co.uk addresses or any of the other variants (for example .org, .net, .info, .biz, .tv, etc.)

rule four
be prepared

Good foundations

If you were ever in the Girl Guides or the Scouts, you may have distant memories of being told to always carry a pocket torch, a Band-Aid and some salt. Being prepared as a Free Agent is a bit more involved, but it will mean you can cope with a lot more than a power cut or a grazed knee.

Preparation is mostly about research and laying good foundations. We have already covered many aspects of the first level of research – knowing yourself – in other chapters. Before you make yourself available for any work, take an inventory of your skills and your availability: you need to know exactly what you're capable of.

As you slip into routines, you'll discover that you work better at certain times of the day than others; alone or with company; at home or in an office. Observing yourself and your working habits objectively will allow to you understand how to offer the best service to your employer or your clients. If you become aware of a weakness in your skillset, now is the time to plug the gap – either by a bit of training or finding another Free Agent to collaborate with. This will enable you to pitch for the widest variety of work, and then carry that work out at a pace and in a manner that suits you.

Although it might be obvious to some, it's worth pointing out that this basic level of research and self-assessment is not something you do as you start out as a Free Agent – it's a process that continues throughout your career. As you become more proficient, confident and well known, your ability and availability will change. As you get to know what you're good at and what you enjoy as a Free Agent, you might also reassess what sort of work or clients you would rather accumulate.

The market

The next level of research involves really getting to know your market. This has many aspects to it – knowing the issues around your industry, the latest developments, the movers and shakers and the trends. The best way to keep on top of this sort of information is by reading any relevant publications – the usual mix of trade newspapers and industry magazines, as well as company newsletters and annual reports if you can get your hands on them. Use your wiles to get on the mailing list of anything you think might be important or useful.

As you are now your own business, you need to act like one. Businesses grow through seizing opportunities, so for Me plc to flourish you also want to read overseas trade magazines so you can spot emerging markets, technologies and stars. Get an overview of anything that might affect the services you offer, or intend to offer. You don't want to see your business taken from you because you didn't adapt soon enough to change.

Very few industries – and therefore Free Agents – are unaffected by changes in technology. So you might want to include in your monthly order from the newsagent a title that keeps you informed about software, networking and hardware developments that could benefit either you or your clients.

The next important area of your research is the key people in your industry. Keep press clippings about them, check their company websites for biographies, and try and make out what makes them tick. If you can work out why they are successful, it might help you emulate them. Or it might help you get to know what they look for, what they admire and what they're lacking. All of these pieces of information will help you to get their attention – and maybe their business.

One of the most valuable things you can learn about people is the way they like to be approached. Some people throw letters in the bin, some never answer their phone. Some chief execs like all new ideas to go straight to them, others only want to be fed the best ideas via a select number of trusted lieutenants. If your research sheds any light on the way these hotshots make decisions and the processes they prefer – this will give you a real competitive edge.

Whether you are freelance or an employee, this research is just as valid. Your allegiance is to yourself, whoever you work for, and having these kinds of facts at your fingertips will inform you when the time is right to resign, where the next boom area will be, or which hotshots you need to befriend.

Your clients

This is possibly the most difficult and time-consuming aspect of your research. Once you have identified the people or companies you want to work for or with, find out as much information about the way they operate as you can. On top of your general market research, find out who the best people are to talk to, if they shut down for summer (no point in calling them then) or if they only offer new contracts at the start of a financial year (no point approaching them before April). Find out too what the company's attitude to Free Agents is – do they use freelancers, do they pay contributors promptly, do they ever give outsiders a chance (some companies seem only to give jobs to existing employees)?

Your reading might tell you if the company is in good shape, if it needs a new product to be more inviting to takeover bids, or if its coffers are full and ripe for investment. But as you can't always believe what you read in the press, call your contacts to check facts that may have a bearing on whom you call and when you call them.

What you're trying to do in this process is really to get to know and understand your clients. Ideally, get yourself into a position where you can anticipate their needs before they do. Maybe if you suggest a new product or practice to them, you can transform their business as well as your own – this will guarantee their gratitude which will hopefully come in the form of more work and new contracts.

Your rivals

Your preliminary research will also help you identify your rivals and potential rivals. Your rivals may be other Free Agents, but may also be small companies and agencies.

Don't feel bullied by bigger rivals – you don't have their overheads so you can undercut their fees.

Get as much information together about your rivals as possible – and you may have to be sneaky to get it. First of all find out how good they are, so ask around your contacts to see if people are satisfied with their work and their levels of service. Discover what their strengths are and identify ways you can capitalize on their weaknesses.

Find out exactly what services they offer, *and* what they don't. Have they got so much work on their books that they're turning away business? Or are they struggling to pay their rent? Then ask yourself how you can improve on their services – you should always be on the lookout for a new angle.

The one piece of information you absolutely have to find out is how much they charge. A sneaky way of doing this is by phoning up – or getting a friend to phone up – and pretend to be a potential customer. Find out how easy they are to do deal with, how quickly they could start work for you, if they can send you an information pack or give you extra information about their products. If you're feeling really sneaky, ask if you could speak to some of their clients to get a reference and see if you can find out any more (and maybe make a useful contact in the process!).

All this will enable you to be prepared for one very important question – how much do *you* charge? The only way to give a correct answer to this question is by knowing what your market value is, and you can only know that after you've done your research. Once you know what the market rate for your skills is, how rare your skills are, and what value for money you represent to a client, only then can you be sure you're charging the right rate. It will provide the basis of all your negotiations with clients and employers.

Get ready

A big part of your preparations should involve making sure that you have everything you need to start work. If you need raw materials to make a product, make sure you have ordered the right quantity. If you need to complete another job before you start the next, make sure it's out of the way. If you're going to have your nose to the grindstone for the next few weeks and won't be surfacing for air – then get to the supermarket and stock up on teabags and tinned food! If you're the sort of person who can't work in a mess, then tidy up the night before you're scheduled to start work. Even if all you require to produce your work is peace and quiet, you still have to ensure that you'll get what you need in adequate quantities.

If you're going to be working on a complicated project – possibly working with other Free Agents or outside agencies – then your preparations will include liaising with your partners. Your diaries need to tally – if you can't start a piece of work until a partner supplies you with certain goods or information, then you must clearly communicate to that partner what their deadline is. Contrary to the dictionary definition, preparation is not something you do before you start work – it's something you continue doing throughout the project.

Whether you are pitching for work or have already won the contract, make sure you've fully understood the brief. If you've been handed a written brief, study it carefully. If it's simply a verbal brief, don't shy away from calling the person commissioning you to make sure that you fully understand what they want. There's no point running away with clever ideas and solutions if you haven't dealt with the basic issues that you've been told need covering. Many mistakes are made by speed-reading documents or assuming you understand a problem (and therefore don't really listen to the detail of what's required). These are the mistakes of amateurs and are mistakes Free Agents can't afford to make.

Put yourself in the shoes of whoever's hiring you.

Work out what they need – it might not be what they're telling you. Maybe they need to hold on to their job, or secure a promotion. Making your client look good may be the best way of clinching the deal. If they're overstretched, what they might need primarily is convenience, or a guarantee that you will meet deadlines. Don't take things at face value – take some time to work out what's really required.

The final piece of preparation brings us back down to Brownie level – if you're going to a meeting somewhere you've never been before, leave enough time to get there. Make sure you've charged your mobile phone, installed the right software on your laptop or picked up enough business cards. Check you don't have lipstick on your teeth or breakfast in your moustache. You are your own marketing campaign – don't blow your chances over something stupid.

rule five
be reliable

Deadlines

Every Free Agent should strive to have a reputation for reliability. As a contractor – that's what we all are now – it's essential that you meet your contractual obligations. That means being as good as you promised you would be and delivering your work when you said you would.

Observing deadlines should become not just second nature to you, but essential nature. Deadlines are one of the mechanisms that let business and commerce operate with any degree of success. Without them, we would not work for profit; we would toil without reward or grace.

There is one thing you need to know about deadlines from the outset: they are cowards.

Deadlines are pack animals that are rarely seen alone.

They hunt in pairs if not in herds. Be warned: a poorly managed deadline can deliver a savage attack on your reputation by sneaking up on you while you're working on something else.

The problem with deadlines is that we work towards them. A deadline might be set for two months hence, and even though there might only be two days' work to do, humans somehow just can't quite manage to motivate themselves to do that work until, say, precisely two days before the deadline. The good thing about deadlines, however, is that without them we would probably never do the work at all.

A key factor in your ability to be reliable will be your ability to manage deadlines. Make sure when you accept a contract that any deadlines connected with it fit in with your existing commitments. If there are clashes, either force yourself to set a false earlier deadline for the other work, or negotiate a different delivery date for the new piece of work.

Often when you are commissioned or instructed to perform a task, the deadline is a bit woolly. You might be asked to deliver something 'in a couple of weeks' time' or 'towards the end of July'. You would do well to cement a date in your mind, always allowing for hiccups, mistakes, computer failure or a postal strike.

Even woolly deadlines must be observed, because once someone is expecting you to deliver your piece of the jigsaw, they may commission other pieces of the jigsaw around that deadline. Or arrange a meeting that would be pointless without your work. A deadline might be movable at the time of commissioning, but at the time of delivery it may very well have become set in stone.

If you know you are going to miss a deadline, it is essential to communicate the delay as soon as possible. You don't want to be the weakest link in anyone else's chain. Just as you expect your post to arrive, your ink cartridges to be in stock and your bus driver not to go on strike, other people are relying on you to deliver on time so they can get on with their day.

Likewise, if there are suppliers you rely on to do your job, you need them to be reliable. If they are not, they make you look bad and may one day lead to you losing a contract or juicy bit of work. So make sure that the people who supply you with the materials you need to do your job are as reliable as you. If they're not – replace them.

While much of being a Free Agent is exciting, deal-making, pushing-yourself, enjoying-yourself stuff, some of it is mundane project management. Whatever we do, we are also project managers. All of us. We all work on a project-by-project basis and those of us who are better project managers are better Free Agents. There are tips and techniques later on in the book (Time Management chapter) about project management skills: these will help you ensure that you always hit the mark and deliver on time.

Quality

One very good reason for negotiating an extension to a deadline is if you realize that the quality your work would suffer without it. A very big part of your reputation for reliability will be borne of your reputation for quality. Often we are tempted as Free Agents whose future is not bound up in the success of the company paying us, to perform to our contractual minimum. This will only work once.

You're only as good as your last piece of work.

As discussed previously, disappointing clients and bosses is one of the most damaging moves a Free Agent can make. If you have led someone to believe that your work will be of a certain standard, then that's what you must deliver if you want to be commissioned again or recommended to anyone else.

If your contract is rolling and you regularly perform the same function or produce the same supply for a company, then maintaining an even standard of work is very important. If you are walking on what appears to be a solid floor, you're not looking for the rotten floorboard that could break your neck. Therefore every floorboard you supply must be as reliable as the last.

Availability

If you are working alone, there is no one to cover for you – or even answer your phone – when you're out at lunch or on the school run. So if you've just emailed an important piece of work to a client before popping out assuming everything is OK, you will miss the call that tells you the email corrupted and asks you to send the work again. If you don't get the message, your client may have a stress-induced heart attack before you're able to resend the email. A big part of reliability is availability and so you need to find ways that enable you to respond to queries and firefight when necessary. Thankfully, technology can help you.

First, you manage expectations by telling clients that you will be away on such and such a date or unavailable between 3 pm and 5 pm. This way the onus is on them to work around your timetable. Email all your clients a few days before you go away. Use technology to your advantage: get voicemail rather than an answerphone so that no one ever gets the engaged tone. Make sure your message says that you pick up messages regularly, or that in emergencies they should try the mobile – anything that can communicate your availability without actually talking to them. All of this will help your image as a reliable Free Agent.

When you are away from your desk, make sure your mobile is charged and switched on. Always carry your contacts book or PDA, and possibly even your laptop with the relevant files on it. If you are truly uncontactable, then make sure your voicemail message conveys this: never leave a client waiting for a callback they're never going to get.

Health

It's stating the obvious, but you clearly can't do good and timely work if you are not well. You therefore need to take very good care of yourself. It's easy as a Free Agent never to take a break. When the work is coming in it's hard to turn it away – especially as you're unlikely to get holiday pay. It's also always tempting to take on extra little projects at the last minute when you can work from anywhere because – unlike employees who probably don't get paid overtime – Free Agents can see a direct financial benefit from working late.

And when you are under the weather it can be hard to stop. It's not like you can phone in sick. You don't even get sick pay. And if you can work from your sick bed, then you may as well work. Which means you might not give yourself a chance to recover. But it's impossible to be reliable if you're constantly under the weather. So eat well, take a bit of exercise, and work some relaxation time into your schedule. It's as important as working time.

If you have contracts that require constant maintenance, you should think about how you supply holiday cover. Maybe you could do some extra work in advance or on your return. You may have to think about finding a stand-in, either someone to whom you can subcontract the job or another Free Agent in your field who can cover your holidays if you cover theirs. If you can't provide this level of service then you may lose contracts to operators who can.

In reality though, few things in working life are so important that they can't be moved by a day or two, or even a week or two. So if you need to take a break, then take it. You might lose one bit of work by taking time off, but at least you'll be in a fit state to deal with all your other clients. Most companies and projects are bigger than the people they employ and can function – at least temporarily – with some of the team missing. The secret is clear communication, which is the foundation of reliability.

rule six
be responsive

Use your advantage

One of the great advantages you have as a Free Agent is your ability to change direction and respond to developments quickly. Big companies are very slow at making changes, either because changes are made at board level and the board only meets twice a year, or because the people who make the decisions aren't those witnessing change on the frontline.

As you are on the frontline *and* in the boardroom of Me plc, you can decide to do something different in the morning and start putting it into practice before lunch. Your willingness to capitalize on opportunities that others can't respond to will be the trait that singles you out for ever-growing success.

Even as an employee, this is extremely relevant. If you become aware that your company is missing a trick, you have the chance either to be responsible for your company plugging the gap in its repertoire (and getting the credit), or leaving. You can either set up on your own, or move to another company which your research tells you will better survive the new challenges you've identified.

The kinds of changes you need to respond to could come from any quarter. They might be political, for example, the terrorist attacks on New York and Washington and the subsequent military action which impacted greatly on airlines and insurers. Or the changes might be economic, like the introduction of the euro, or tax increases or removals of certain duties. More than likely at some stage they'll be technological, either because 3G mobile phones let your customers access you from anywhere in the country, or because a rival has found a way of manufacturing your product faster and cheaper.

The other advantage you have over big companies is that – because you are prepared and have done your research – you are well versed in every sector that has an impact on your own. In big companies, the guy in marketing knows about changes that impact on the marketing strategy while the guy in sales knows about changes in the sales market. Only when they meet do they get to share that information. As you are at the centre of your own research matrix, you will be in a position to spot trends few others can.

A Free Agent can respond to a trend before anyone else even knows it exists.

Be smart

Part of being responsive is having somewhere else to go. If your knowledge has specialized to the point that you don't know about anything else, you are extremely vulnerable to outside changes. The web designer who only learnt to code HTML was suddenly unemployable when clients started demanding sites built with Flash software. Specializing yourself into a cul-de-sac isn't smart, and it's very easy to avoid.

The best Free Agents always combine their skills. They might write and teach. Or make music and sell music. Or combine contacts with knowledge. You have to be prepared for one of your areas of knowledge to either become common knowledge (and therefore not worth paying for) or redundant (ditto), so be smart and make sure

you have another string to your bow or another punch in your repertoire.

This rule especially extends to your contacts. If you rely on one individual for your information or your contracts, what happens if they retire or step under the proverbial bus? To use the cliché – don't put all your eggs in one basket.

Of course, it's not just industries and current affairs that change. Your circumstances are bound to change as well. What happens if you have kids, move to another part of the country or just get bored? What do you do then? Can your Free Agency survive?

Living in a permanent state of professional whitewater is as exhausting as it is exhilarating. Not knowing where the money to pay the mortgage in two months' time will come from can be stressful enough, without the added worries of contacts disappearing or your skills becoming redundant. The truth, however, is that employees are just as vulnerable – their benevolent boss could be head-hunted and replaced by a tyrant, or their company's market could dry up. You are no more vulnerable to change as a Free Agent, you're just smart enough to be aware of your vulnerability. Corporate drones might appear to have security, but it's just a false sense of security. As a Free Agent, you have to accept that you will have good months and scary months.

You are now on a career rollercoaster, not a ladder.

So what would happen if you started a family or moved abroad? The truth is you could adapt much more quickly as a Free Agent than as an employee. You can take on more or less work to suit your needs and availability. If you're responsive you will cope – only a blinkered or stick-in-the-mud attitude can stop you from incorporating any life change into your Free Agency. If you are not responsive, your Free Agency will not survive. Or, as they say in Clichéville, you have a choice – adapt or die.

On the job

Sometimes – if not often – a client's circumstances or needs can change in the middle of a contract and you have to respond immediately. This can put you in a difficult position and you need to know how you'll respond. For instance, you may have quoted to carry out a task based on the assumption that it would take you five days to do it. Your client's change of heart midway through now means it will take you eight days. How much of the cost can you pass on?

If you negotiate the right terms at the beginning of the job, this should be easy. Your client should know that for any changes to the brief after the agreement has been made they will incur an extra cost. If your client is your boss, then your boss needs to take some of your other responsibilities off your hands, or extend the deadline for completion. As a Free Agent you never do anything for free. You might do something as a favour, on the understanding the favour will be returned one day. Or out of curiosity so that you might learn something new. But you never do anything for free. Make sure you are happy with the pay-off.

Assuming the cost has been met by your client and your other work can be fitted in around the revised job, you now have to deal with the changes. Can you? Do you have the supplies, the stomach and the heart to complete the job? As a Free Agent you should always be able to respond to these sorts of challenges. You should always expect some changes to be made to any project and you'd be wise to timetable in enough time to accommodate changes when you work out your fee. This has the added benefit of making you appear to be in control, or that you handled an extra piece of work for the same price. The truth is, if they hadn't made the change you would have been paid for work that never had to be done. Smart.

What if – worst-case scenario – the change of brief involves the cancellation of the project and you will either not get paid, or not get paid as much as you had budgeted for? In this sort of situation you want to see if you have a secondary market for your work, or ensure you get compensated (ideally financially, but maybe in some other way). You certainly need to be sure that you have financial reserves in place.

Good grace

Whatever the change in circumstances, embrace it with good grace. Imagine you've worked out that your company's market is shrinking and you pipe up in a meeting with your bosses to pronounce doom and gloom, then you won't be very popular. If, on the other hand, you spot that you can avoid market collapse by adopting a new procedure or product, announcing this in a meeting will energize the meeting, and mark you out as an optimistic, energetic and valuable person.

When you're in the middle of a project it can be particularly distressing to have a client or boss criticize or ask for changes, but this is what being in business is like. If you're in a shop buying a jumper, you ask if they stock it in other colours or sizes – and that's all your client is doing. Think of your clients as customers and try to keep them satisfied. A sulky face or an easily bruised ego are not the kind of accessories that are going to help you win future contracts.

Change isn't bad, it's inevitable. You just have to make sure that you deal with it efficiently and professionally. The best way is by anticipating it. Never resist it, always embrace it. As a Free Agent, change is one of the most valuable advantages you have. Use it.

Stephen • 39 • trains expert • Yorkshire

'Can I get one thing straight right at the start,' says Stephen, 'I am not a train spotter. And as a little boy I never once wanted to be a train driver.' Until he was 22, Stephen viewed trains the way most of us do – an unreliable means of transport with a reputation for bad sandwiches.

'I graduated from university at 22 with a useless degree in chemistry and had no idea what to do. I quite fancied the media but the only job I could get was as an editorial assistant on a hobby magazine for trainspotters.' It wasn't his ideal job but he quickly realized that trains had millions of enthusiasts and that working for a trains magazine wasn't quite as limited a niche as he'd first thought and this boring job turned out to be quite an opportunity.

After a few years of answering readers' enquiries about engine sizes and enamel finishes, being sent free copies of books and attending press conferences at rail company headquarters, he was well on his way to becoming a train 'expert'. He was soon promoted and within two years became the magazine's editor.

'My time on the train magazine coincided with the deregulation of the industry so the media always needed a talking head to go on news programmes to talk about the industry. I suppose I became quite well known.' Stephen was able to use his new-found profile to get the interest of publishers who commissioned him to write books about trains and the history of railways.

After he left the magazine Stephen was amazed to find out how valuable his specialist knowledge was. 'National newspapers asked me to write the occasional feature for them, some even sent me overseas to write about the bullet trains in Japan and the TGVs in France. Suddenly writing about trains seemed very glamorous!'

Seventeen years since he grudgingly took his first job, Stephen now makes a fine Free Agent living from trains. 'My regular source of income is from lecturing. The railways were so important to history in the nineteenth and twentieth centuries that there is always a course somewhere in Britain that needs my knowledge.' As well as lecturing, Stephen still writes books that sell well worldwide. 'I quite often travel abroad to promote the books – believe me it's a nice life!' And as an additional source of income, one anonymous merchant bank keeps him on a retainer as an industry analyst to advise them which rail companies and markets to invest in.

'This is not a career I could ever have imagined for myself when I was younger,' he says. 'And if I had stayed on staff at the magazine I'd not have had the time to do the other things I've done – and I would only be earning about a fifth of what I do now. The thing I really, really enjoy about my work is that people are always asking me for my opinion. I'm trusted to give the right information because my clients know that I really know my stuff. I know more about steam engines than any sane person ought to know, but my specialist knowledge lets me charge a higher day-rate.'

rule seven
be brave

Rewards, not awards

Being brave doesn't always mean being stupid. It doesn't always involve taking risks. Being brave is sometimes about doing difficult things, or being first, or sometimes it's just saying 'no'. Or 'yes'. Many of the things you will find yourself undertaking as a Free Agent will involve a degree of bravery.

Setting out on your own – whether that's setting up your own business or simply taking responsibility for the future direction of your career – is brave. Most people never take that kind of control of their lives because they don't want the responsibility of failure. Then again, most people can't wait until it's time to go home, or to the pub. Most people don't really live.

This is your reward as a Free Agent – you get to be truly alive.

You get to use every brain cell, every character trait, everything you've ever learnt. You will feel empowered, positive and optimistic. Even if you never earn any more money than you did before, this is your handsome reward for bravery. Many people talk about getting awards for their bravery – a badge from someone else – rather than the simple, and ample, rewards that are inherent in being the best you can be.

There will be times as a Free Agent when you'll find yourself doing something you have never done before – maybe taking on an order twice as big as anything you've handled previously, or working for a blue-chip client, or using a recently acquired skill. As an employee, taking new steps is easier for two reasons: first, you would never be given a new project or role unless your boss believed you could do it; and second, there's usually someone around egging you on or holding your hand. As a Free Agent, only you can egg yourself on; you have to shout encouragement from your own sideline.

You won't always feel like being this 'up'. Whether you've had bad news or a dose of the flu, there will be days when you just want to stay in bed. The good news is that as a portfolio worker you don't have to be brave every day. There will always be an easy client to deal with, or you can legitimately spend a morning sorting out your receipts instead of hustling for work. Mostly, you only have to be brave when you feel like it. This makes bravery a lot easier.

Carpe diem

Your bravery is the mechanism that drives your career forward. Without it you wouldn't have a career outside corporate life. If you weren't brave, you wouldn't have considered becoming a Free Agent – so even if you consider yourself timid, you are probably already braver than you know.

The trick with bravery is seizing your moment.

Timing can make you a hero.

Just being alert to opportunity can open a door for you that others don't even know exists. But are you brave enough to open it? To go where others have never been? Or even just somewhere you've never been? If you're the kind of person that likes pushing themselves or who indulges in the thrill of the new, then this isn't going to be a problem for you. But what if you're naturally introverted, or just unsure?

The thing with bravery is that it's not always a win/lose situation. It's more win/stay the same. Seizing a new opportunity isn't gambling with everything you hold dear. More often than not it's just a way of adding to your repertoire, CV, or even just your dinner party repartee. You mustn't think that bravery always involves risk.

Sometimes though, there is a serious risk involved. It might be leaving a regular salary, it might be taking out a loan, or it might be compromising a relationship to follow a dream. So how do you deal with that? Some people choose the pros and cons list option. Or toss a coin. Others turn to a tabloid horoscope for a clue. Others ask a complete stranger. Over time, rest assured, taking these sorts of decisions will become easier.

There are no guarantees with risks – except the one that proves the rule. And the rule is that all successful people have taken a risk. Risk avoidance is the route of dissatisfaction, or compromise and maybe even of failure. You're not guaranteed success every time you take a risk, but you are guaranteed disappointment every time you walk away from bravery.

There are, of course, some risks that aren't worth taking. Like gambling your home the week before the baby's due. But as long as you are prepared to lose your stake, every risk – every act of bravery – is a win/win situation. Either you get the desired result, or you get knowledge and experience that will mean you do better next time.

Over time, you will come to accept risk as part of your working day. You'll no longer see walking up to your boss with a crazy new plan as a moment that could lead to embarrassment – you'll only see it as another door to another opportunity. And if the door doesn't open, you won't even mind because you know there'll be another one tomorrow. Or next week. Even the most demure of Free Agents will come to see risk as an integral part of their working day – like the photocopier or meetings.

Heroism

Sometimes professional bravery requires you to be somebody else's hero. That might mean going into the office at midnight to sort out a problem or going the extra mile to get something in on time. It might just be holding the fort in times of stress. Or calling in a favour for a contact.

Just like wars need heroes, so too do businesses and industries. Certainly the trade press needs heroes (they are far more interesting for journalists to write about). If you can occasionally go beyond bravery into heroism, you can give your career an enormous boost. Exceeding clients' expectations is always a smart move, but if you save their necks it's far more likely they will give you work again, pay you more or recommend you with enthusiasm. And if you do something really spectacular, it might get a mention in your trade publication. That will certainly boost your profile and your business.

Joanna • 30 • hospitality manager • London

When Jo's boss asked her to participate in a senior management team-building exercise, she was flattered, but a bit apprehensive. It was great to be considered important enough to attend, but she also knew that any weekend away with her colleagues would involve lots of alcohol, followed by plenty of machismo and bragging. At 25 she might have seen it as an opportunity to get noticed and get ahead, but at 30 she was bored with her male colleagues hitting on her. However, as it was compulsory she got in her company car on Friday afternoon and drove to a country house hotel in the middle of Wiltshire. When she arrived she discovered that all the other senior women in the company were attending the same course the following weekend. She was to be the only woman in a group of 25.

This didn't really bother her until the following day when the group was put through their paces on an army assault course. 'I knew myself well enough to know I didn't have to walk on tightropes or spend four hours soaking wet to feel good about my work,' remembers Jo. As the day went on, some of the men on the course – including her chief executive – got more and more boisterous as the adrenaline starting pumping. While they abseiled, Jo simply held the ropes – and effectively her colleagues' lives in her hands.

At the end of the day they returned to the hotel and Jo ran herself a bath before dinner with her colleagues. 'I lay in that bath and thought, "Not one of them asked me if I was enjoying myself." They hadn't noticed that I really didn't care who climbed walls fastest or recoiled at their incessant chants of "faster, better, more" as they tried to impress the boss.'

She realized that the behaviour displayed on the assault course was an exaggerated version of the office politics she faced every day. Because her chief exec never handed out praise, each of his subordinates was forced to blow their own trumpet to let anyone know of their achievements. This led to all sorts of rivalries and in-fighting. Realizing that she worked in an unsupportive and aggressive environment, *she decided to resign*. She didn't need her boss to tell her she was good, she knew she was and was confident she wouldn't be without work for long.

At dinner that night she was seated next to her boss, an extremely tall American who had played football at college. He was huge, loud and intimidating. 'So Jo,' he asked, 'what do you think of this course then?'

She proceeded to tell him. She had nothing to lose but a job she no longer wanted. She told him that he had poorly motivated staff who didn't feel rewarded or valued, she told him that he never asked for anyone else's opinion and ran the company like a dictatorship.

Others overheard and added their grievances. Before long the six-foot-four-inch bully was in tears. 'But I work with the best team in the business,' he said. 'If I didn't think they were any good I would sack them.' It then dawned on him that saying 'good work' to a competent and enthusiastic employee was cheaper than paying a head-hunter to replace them.

At work the following week, things were immediately different. The chief exec started inviting department heads into his office to seek counsel. He even phoned them himself rather than getting his secretary to summon them. Staff were praised and given credit. And Jo stayed after he told her how much he respected her.

'As soon as I had made the decision to leave, I became his equal,' Jo says now. 'One of the rules in my career now is to be ready to go. I may work for a salary but I'm a Free Agent, free to leave or to get my rewards in other ways. If I hadn't been prepared to confront my boss, then I certainly would have been out of that job: after that weekend I simply could not have stayed.'

rule eight
be happy

Don't do it if it don't do it for you

You might think that 'being happy' should be more a by-product of Free Agency, rather than one of its founding commandments. But if Free Agency is not making you happy, then you really should be thinking about getting a proper job. Or just accepting the faults and pressures of your existing one.

Free Agency isn't about getting rich or being the next Richard Branson – it's about getting happy.

If not knowing what you're going to be doing next week, uncertain cashflow, and pressure from clients make you so tense you've neither fingernails nor hair left, perhaps Free Agency isn't for you. If your company has decided your new enthusiasm is unwanted and that you're a trouble-maker, then maybe for the time being you should play the corporate game or switch companies. If the benefits of setting your own timetable and being your own boss don't outweigh the stresses, then you'd better get used to your commute, your boss and your office politics.

But that doesn't mean it's for everyone, and if it's not for you then pass this book on to someone else. Life's too short to adopt strategies and rules that make you unhappy, stop you sleeping or make you too ratty to live with. You've got to expect occasional short-term hiccups, bad patches and stress. But if Free Agency has turned you into a chronic worrier and is making you miserable, then there's no shame in going back to the 9 to 5.

Free Agency might only work for you in part, or for some of the time. It might be that you just need to make use of some of the rules or some of the tools outlined in this book: Free Agency doesn't have to be all or nothing. Perhaps just taking a bit more responsibility or learning to sell yourself a bit harder will be all you need to do to get more out of your working day.

Six ways to happiness

There are many ways that Free Agency can help you find happiness through work. It's important to recognize how each one can lead to your professional fulfilment and happiness.

- **Pride**
  Being proud of what you do, whom you work for, how well you do your work, and the results you achieve, fills anyone with a sense of well-being. If you can't be proud of what you do, your conscience may never let you be truly happy in your work.
- **Love**
  You should love what you do. Either love the people you work with, the process of working, the results you achieve or just the subject matter you immerse yourself in. On bad days it will never be hard to remember why you get up in the morning, answer the phone or switch on the computer.
- **Satisfaction**
  Even on your shittiest, nastiest projects, the feeling of completing them with flair and grace can (almost) remove the memories of the worst days and worst aspects of the job. Taking a step back

and knowing that you were the best you could be – and did the best you could do – produces powerful feelings of happiness and relief.

- **Cheap thrills**
  Sometimes the perks can make it all worthwhile. The gadget you were given at a conference, the upgrade to business class, or the opportunity to get one over on a rival all legitimately produce a smile. You might not have enjoyed the work, but at least you got to stay in a nice hotel! We're all suckers for a nice freebie – enjoy them!

- **Money**
  The love of money might be the root of all evil, but money itself can certainly buy a lot of good. And goodies. Let's not get too hippy here – we all love the stuff and we're all happier when we've got more of it. There's no finer way to start the day than by opening the post to find a few cheques. A successful Free Agent always looks forward to the post arriving! It should be fun earning money as a Free Agent, but not as much fun as spending it!

- **Freedom**
  The path to happiness is paved with freedom. On bad days, just remember how important your freedom is. You're slaving away for yourself. You are your own master. Few workers ever have that – remember that and relish it.

Smile and dial!

This bit of being happy is more of an instruction than a rule. No one wants to work with a miserable, moaning, droning bore. You're going to find it very hard to find work if you're no fun to be with. But not as hard as getting repeat business if you take your personal black cloud with you to meetings or into the office.

If you are feeling down, find a way to gee yourself up a bit before you get on the phone and pitch for business or talk to a client. As the Yanks say – smile and dial!

Part of your personal brand has to be that you are the kinda guy people like to have around. This doesn't mean that you have to crack jokes, just that you're pleasant, amenable and sensitive to the office around you. Only the very very brilliant can get away with being morose and difficult. Every Free Agent is an actor who can take on a variety of roles. And like an actor, you have to be able to give 'em what they want. And they wants happy. Better go and buy some tooth-whitening toothpaste!

Jamal • 32 • structural engineer • Edinburgh

On the face of it, Jamal is a classic corporation guy. He's held the same job with the same firm for six years. He doesn't particularly enjoy it, but he's paid extremely well. And because he's trusted and treated as part of the furniture, he's left to monitor his own work with little interference or supervision.

'I have a deal with my boss that as long as my work continues to be of good enough quality, I meet my deadlines and carry on getting on with my colleagues, then he won't ask any questions,' says Jamal.

For the past four years Jamal has worked Saturdays and taken Mondays off. He's often missing for large chunks of the day, at other times of the week as well but always makes sure he's at the end of a mobile for emergencies. So, what is he doing when his colleagues are filling the time until 6 pm? He's wheeling and dealing in the property market, that's what.

In 1998 he bought his first rental investment. With the help of his financial adviser he took £30,000 equity out of his home (his mortgage went up by about £150 a month) to use as a deposit on the new property which he bought with a buy-to-let mortgage. The repayments would be covered by rent. As he was already in the highest tax bracket, he didn't want to earn an income from the property because so much of it would go to the taxman. So he arranged a 15-year term on the new mortgage, which meant by the time he was 43 he would own the flat outright. Assuming he had paid off his own mortgage at this stage he could live in his own house while living off the rental income from the new property. He wouldn't have to work.

It was too easy. All that capital growth *and* a monthly income? He decided to do it again. Four years on he now owns five buy-to-let properties and his property portfolio is worth close to £1million. 'I've been very lucky. The property market has performed very well in Edinburgh in that time, both for sales and lettings.' Obviously, property markets slump as well as soar and he's aware that a recession could leave him out of pocket. 'If that happens I can simply sell one of the properties to shore up the others. Over time though, the property market has always out performed almost any other type of investment: as long as I can be flexible about when I sell I should be OK.' And as a single man without kids he has the luxury of such bravery.

What he discovered from his dabbling in property was that (a) he was good at it and (b) he loved it. He is now planning to leave engineering behind and move into property full time. 'I'm going to work as an estate agent for a year, to make contacts and to learn a bit more about the business. After that I plan to build the portfolio, taking money out of one property to pay for the next.' As well as renting, Jamal also intends to get into renovations. 'Since I've been going to auctions I can see a gap in the market – big developers are only interested in property they can make £50,000–£100,000 on. I'd be happy to make £40k. A couple of those a year and I'll be laughing!'

Like so many Free Agents, Jamal found that what made him rich was also a hobby that made him happy.

02

part two
the tools

Now you know about the rules of Free Agency, it's time to get to grips with the essential tools every Free Agent needs for success. You will learn why they are important and how to incorporate them into any working situation. Living by the rules and using the Tools is the smartest way to operate as a Free Agent.

tools one
networking

Contacts, contacts, contacts

If the three most important things to consider when buying a property are location, location, location, then the equivalent for Free Agency is contacts, contacts, contacts.

Contacts are the most valuable commodity in Free Agent Nation. The more you have, the richer you are. Contacts equal opportunity, influence and ready access to knowledge. So how many have you got? And how many more are you going to have by the end of the week?

Networking is a pretty nasty word – it sounds like something computers do rather than people. However, it's an accurate description of the process by which we acquire and use our contacts. Like it or not, networking is something you're going to have to get good at. So let's look at how you get contacts, how you maintain them, and how you use them.

Creating a network

Before you start worrying about not having enough – or any – contacts and fretting about how you're going to 'work the room' at the next event you attend, it's worth looking at who you already know. You might be surprised to realize who you've already got in your contacts book.

As we've discussed previously, a contact is not just someone you know, they are also a link to other contacts. You have to start to see yourself at the centre of an entire web of contacts: you might not know all the people in the web, but you know someone who knows someone who knows someone. And even if the people you know aren't directly 'useful' to you, the people they have in their contacts book may be. So although you might not personally be on first-name terms with influential people in your field, you might well have a relationship with someone who is.

You might also find that your friends and family are better connected than you've ever realized. Their buddies might work for a company that's of interest to you or perhaps they went to university with someone who studied something that's of use to you. A contact is not necessarily someone you get to know through work, it might be someone you've met at dinner or in the pub. Ask to be put in touch with them.

For many people starting out in their careers, the most valuable network they have are the people they went to school or college with. If you took a vocational course, the chances are that most of your classmates went into similar jobs after graduation. On graduation, your network immediately swells exponentially from being the 30 people in your class to *all* the people working with those 30 people – all of whom now work in the same or allied fields. The smartest and easiest network you'll ever use simply involves hanging on to the people you already know. Whether you were at university together for years or only came together for an evening class or weekend training, make sure you never finish a course without getting everyone's phone number and email address.

Some colleges have official alumni networks. These do everything from encouraging graduates to work together at preferential rates to sending out newsletters keeping members abreast of promotions and appointments.

Alumni associations were once for squares and nerds; now they're serious business tools.

If it has been several years since you graduated or left school, it can still be worth getting in touch with old classmates. Many colleges and schools operate unofficial 'old boy' and 'old girl' networks and FriendsReunited.co.uk provides email addresses for people you went to school with. It's amazing how useful some of these 'dead' contacts can be. And it might also be fun to hook up with your old friends.

If you are in a job, your contacts include everyone you work with – and consequently everyone they've ever worked with. Often when you start a new job in the same field, there will be people in the new company who have worked with people you know. Use this link to introduce yourself and make even more contacts.

Often your best contacts aren't sitting at the next desk – they are at the other end of the phone. Advertising sales people always need to develop good relationships with marketers and advertising agencies, and journalists always need to befriend press officers. People who work in symbiotic industries to your own – as a general rule – make the best contacts. Not only do you both need each other, which always expedites any transaction, but they will also know your opposite number in other companies. These kinds of contacts make very good spies and informants. After contacts, the next most valuable commodity is knowledge.

Broaden your horizons

Ideally you want to have a good spread of contacts. If your contacts are all in one area, then you will always be walking towards the same horizon. If contacts are opportunities, then you really want to make sure you have a contact in every sector of your industry.

If you imagine for a moment that your company is your entire industry, let's think about the contacts you need. You want to get to know everyone from the IT guy to the mailroom guy, to the man that lets you park your car on the sly, to the boss's PA, to the boss, to the receptionist. We haven't even started talking about your colleagues and the people you will work with on deals and projects.

A contact then, is anyone who can help you get what you want, ideally faster and more accurately than you could on your own. You also need a broad base of contacts ranging from people who you need to do things for you (like the IT guy) to the people who make decisions about the direction your company will take (like the boss) and who can give you some inside information.

Outside of your company, you want actively to develop contacts in an equally broad range of fields. If you work in computer manufacturing, get to know people in hardware, software, processing, sales, etc. It might also be useful to get to know a journalist on a computer magazine or join a users' group so you get to know your end users. Only knowing other people in your department or narrow field will guarantee that you stay there. A well-connected Free Agent is a successful one.

If you've never had a hobby before, you do now: you're a contact collector.

Throughout your career you want to connive and contrive to put yourself in situations where you will make new contacts. Whether that's your high school reunion or joining your union, you want to find as many ways of networking as possible. Or it might just be talking to people in lifts when you're in a 'useful' building or taking on additional work just because it will bring you into contact with new people.

Tips for networking

Whatever stage you're at in your career, you need to maintain and expand your network of contacts. Whether you 'meet' people on the phone or at conferences and exhibitions, many of the techniques are the same.

Introduce yourself

This is one of the most basic rules of networking, and yet so many people forget to do it. When you start a new job or contract, use this as an opportunity to go round the office saying hello. And don't just tell people your name, tell them why you're there. Are you working on Project X or taking over from someone else? And while you're letting everyone know who you are and what you do, make sure you find out their names and job function and find out if there are ways you can work together or share information. When you make contacts on the phone always make sure they get to know you as Joe Bloggs, not Joe from the Acme Corp. otherwise when you leave Acme Corp. your name will mean very little to your contacts. After all, you're Joe from the Joe Bloggs Corp. now.

Go to conferences

Or parties. Or exhibitions. Or anywhere where people you need to meet congregate. Sometimes they can be expensive and as a Free Agent you may not have a boss who will foot the bill, but there are often several ways you can attend these events at a reduced cost. Maybe one of the people exhibiting or speaking could invite you? Maybe you could do some work in exchange for a ticket? Maybe – if you're good at blagging – you'll find some way of sneaking in (pretending to be a journalist and asking for a press pass can sometimes work!). When you're there, always wear a name badge. You might feel like a bit of a lemon, but it's a good way for people to introduce themselves to you – and you never know, there might be someone there who is looking out just for you!

Get introductions

It can be daunting and frightening turning up at an event where you don't know anyone, so do your groundwork before you arrive. Tell the conference organizer that you'd really like to meet so-and-so while you're there, and get them to make the introduction when you arrive. If you do know people, get them to introduce you to all the people *they* know. This instantly gives you credibility and makes you more memorable to the person you're introduced to. Alternatively, when you sign the guest book at any event, see who's already signed in. If there's someone there you want to meet, ask the host to make the introduction.

Be interested and interesting

When you do get talking to someone new, really pay attention. Listen intently and make eye contact. Ask them why they're there and who they know. If you forget their name at the end of the conversation, ask for their card – and always make sure that you give them yours. And remember, when you are talking to them, don't bore them. Find something memorable or pertinent to say about the event you're attending. And be pleasant. No one likes a jerk.

Always carry your business card

Whether you're going to dinner with friends, to a meeting or to the match, never be without a few cards in your pocket. You never know when you're going to meet someone useful. Some people use their business card to make a statement – either it's made of luminous plastic or doubles as a CD-ROM – but this isn't necessary. What's important is that you use it as a valuable advertising opportunity. A business card shouldn't just say who you are, but what you do.

Maintaining your network

Once you've developed a network, as well as expanding it you also need to maintain it. After all, there's no point in going to the effort and expense of making contacts if you're not going to hold on to them. First, you need to make sure that you store your contacts' details efficiently. That might be a Rolodex of business cards or electronically stored on your PDA – however you do it, make sure you keep a back-up. If you lose your Palm or a virus corrupts your hard drive you will lose the single most valuable thing you own. And if you keep your contacts in an address book, make sure you photocopy the pages every six months or so.

If you have just met someone at a conference, as soon as you get back to your desk send him or her an email saying how much you enjoyed meeting them. Include in that email an offer to help them out – make it clear that they can contact you. If you discussed something memorable – like a particular speaker or piece of kit – forward any additional information you've since found out on that topic. If you said you would do something for them – like dig out a press clipping or forward someone else's details, make sure you do that. And if someone suggests meeting up, reply with the dates you are available.

One of the best ways of maintaining your network is also one of the best ways of adding value to it. If you meet someone who could benefit from meeting someone you already know, arrange to get them together. Establish yourself as someone who knows people and can make things happen.

Start looking out for your contacts. If you read something that would be useful to them, pass it on. Or if you read about them, get in touch to congratulate them on the article. If they get a promotion – send a card or an email. All this will make it much easier when you contact them asking for help, or just asking if they know anyone who can help you.

Sometimes contacts slip and go cold; getting in touch in these situations can seem inappropriate or embarrassing. Often just reminding a contact how you met will be enough to get their grey matter working, but the best way of renewing old contacts is by bumping into them again. So keep attending industry events, or going to parties or speeches after work, just so you can keep your contacts as hot as possible.

Maintaining contacts is about equal amounts of backscratching. Reciprocation may not be immediate, but after years of working in the same field as each other, you will have an even number of favours called in by both parties. And as you get better known and more influential, the chances are that the Not Very Important Contact you made ten years ago is now your main link to work and opportunity. So even if someone's business card declares them to be the Paperclip Manager, they are still worth curating in your contact collection. If you think they're smart and savvy, the chances are that in a few years' time the Paperclip Manager will be the CEO.

MEET THE AGENTS

Dominic • 42 • systems consultant • Luton

Dominic worked for 12 years in the systems department of a merchant bank in London. He started as a middleweight techie, slowly being promoted to manage the department, and then the division across Europe. 'I'd never meant to stay in one company so long, but working on systems for a bank is about as exciting as systems gets!' And as they kept promoting him and giving him more money he saw no reason to move on.

'As my kids got older however, it became more of a strain on family life that I was always on call for breakdowns or often attending conferences around the world. I knew I had to make a change.' But before he got the chance he was made redundant unexpectedly. It was actually a lucky break. 'There I was thinking about setting up on my own and suddenly I was given a pay-off. It wasn't the most generous package, but I could have been starting off solo with nothing behind me.'

As his departure from corporate life came a little sooner than he'd planned, he started off by approaching a temp agency for an interim income. 'It was my agent there who first suggested becoming a limited company. She told me how to buy a company off the shelf to take advantage of the tax breaks which were available a few years ago.' Although he didn't do much temp work, the agency put him in touch with his accountant who continues to exploit tax law to Dominic's advantage.

The temp agency negotiated a few contracts for him but Dominic still found he was commuting to London most of the week. 'I knew the key to a good life was getting away from maintaining systems to designing them. The work isn't as regular but it pays extremely well.' Dominic started off by simply calling himself a 'systems consultant' rather than a 'systems engineer' and almost immediately he noticed a difference. 'I was so gobsmacked by the change in reception I got from potential clients that it stunned me into realizing success is all about presentation and perception.'

As well as prompting him to invest in a good suit for meetings, Dominic contacted trade magazines covering the systems industry and offered to write for them. He also contacted the organizers of some of the conferences he had been attending for years – some of whom he'd got to know quite well – and volunteered to be a panellist or chairman for some of the sessions they were putting together.

'It felt very arrogant, pushing myself forward like that, but I was actually making their lives easier so I suppose it wasn't that surprising that I got such a good reception.' Dominic used his profile as an industry 'expert' to further his 'consultancy'. And instead of paying to attend conferences, he was being paid to be there!

'I networked like mad and let people know that – finally – I was freelance and available for work.' It didn't happen overnight but the contracts finally trickled in. 'I now do one day a month at a rival bank, as an extremely well-paid consultant keeping them up to date on technology, which I now have time to read about and experiment with.' This knowledge also helps him get the designing contracts he wanted so badly.

'I work for banks all over the world – usually just for a few days for meetings, then the rest of the work is done in my shed. I then subcontract out the installation work and take a retainer for the maintenance contracts. I only need to do one of those a year to earn a very nice living indeed.'

tools two
learning

Learn from everything and everyone

One of the very best things about being a Free Agent is that you have a chance of using everything you've ever learnt. Maybe you read a profile of Jack Welch in a Sunday paper that gave you a bit of sage advice, or maybe your love of Bollywood films might get worked into your daily life somehow. If you can use everything you've ever learnt, then learning itself is a key tool you have to master.

Many are guilty of stopping learning when they reach a certain level or finish a certain course. They think they know certain processes or sectors inside out and they stop there. When this happens, their careers either nose-dive or are greatly foreshortened.

Once you stop learning, you stop being useful.

Thinking that learning has something to do with being taught is an easy mistake to make. You don't just learn when someone tells you something or teaches you a new skill: you learn through observation, experience and sometimes even by osmosis. You need to start learning from everything and everyone. Someone you work with might know a neat trick with Microsoft Word; someone else might be able to teach you how to operate a forklift truck – both of these things are bits of knowledge to be stored and used as and when you need them.

Take a minute to think about what you know. And what you don't know. Try and identify the gaps in your knowledge and your abilities and make sure that your learning involves taking care of your weaknesses. There might be some obvious skill you need to learn or some qualification you could really benefit from. If there is, make this the core of your learning for the foreseeable future.

It might not always be obvious that you've learnt something – one day you might simply have imperceptibly reached a more competent level – so it's important to set aside some regular time to quantify your learning. Otherwise it's too easy to meet someone knowledgeable or read something valuable and move on to the next encounter before you've registered what you've learnt. Just like your times table at school, repeating words of wisdom will help them stick.

Your ability to keep your heart and mind open to new learning will have a direct bearing on your effectiveness and success as a Free Agent. You now need to have a greater range of knowledge and skills so you have to start recognizing useful bits of information as 'learning' and then store them in ways you can use them.

Your sector

The first area of knowledge to cover is your immediate sector. This means reading those trade publications (again!), scouring websites and newsgroups, attending seminars and conferences, reading biographies of significant people in your industry, and buying relevant books on your specialist area.

Get to know about developments, appointments, ongoing research, sales figures and economic data relating to your industry. It's worth keeping a cuttings file of pertinent news clippings as well as filing your notes from any useful seminars. When you attend a seminar you might not necessarily learn anything about the subject, but you

will always learn something about the capability of the speaker, or simply pick up a delegates list so that you can learn other delegates' contact details. This is all valuable learning.

Many industries require you to continue with some kind of formal learning to keep upgrading your skills. Certainly as you climb into managerial positions it may be necessary to learn processes and procedures that you were previously unaware of. As a Free Agent it is crucial that you are as well trained as your PAYE counterparts. Let your contacts tell you which courses are the best and try and negotiate reduced-cost access if you can't persuade your boss or a client to pay (many training companies have private and corporate rates).

Beyond your sector

As well as your specialist knowledge, remember to keep your general knowledge topped up. This means keeping abreast of the latest management thinking or general business trends. It is therefore always worth reading the business pages of your newspaper and occasionally remembering to buy a magazine like *Fast Company* or *The Economist* instead of *Heat*.

You also ideally need to be aware of general economic conditions. For example, how events like the introduction of the euro are affecting Free Agents on the continent, or how new taxation rules could benefit your business. You certainly don't want to be planning expansion in a certain territory if the economic conditions there are poor. So add the finance pages to your reading diet.

Another area of general knowledge you want to plug into from time to time is technology. Very few Free Agents will find that their work isn't made easier or more effective by developments in either software or hardware. Advance knowledge of new products in development might stop you from buying something that's about to become obsolete!

Not only will this kind of general knowledge inform your chit-chat with colleagues and clients; it may also directly influence how you run your Free Agency. Remember, a ship with an even load is more stable and less likely to bank and roll: make sure you're evenly loaded with a good spread of knowledge.

Learn from people

As a Free Agent working on more than one project, you are more likely than most workers to work with a greater number of people.

This significantly increases your opportunities to learn from colleagues and clients. When you find yourself impressed by a speaker, a sales rep or a colleague, take a moment to deconstruct the reasons they made the right impression. Was it what they did, or the way that they did it? Was it their method or their mad ideas that propelled the project forward? Or was it just that they smiled and made eye contact? Sometimes taking a moment to reflect on your professional encounters will reveal gems of wisdom you will never read in a book. Make sure you take the time to do this.

Whether it's an old master or a young buck who's just learnt some new buzzword on an NVQ course, try to learn something from everyone you come into contact with.

Even if you don't work directly with a person who impresses you, you can still learn much from simply observing them. You can note when and how they manage to get the boss's ear, or how they dress, or how long they spend at their desk. All of these things are clues that can help you work out how to perform better in any given situation.

You can still learn from people even if you never meet them. Many leading business figures, athletes, politicians, entertainers and gurus (most of whom will be Free Agents) write autobiographies from which you can glean hard-learnt wisdom. Stories of how the successful worked for that success or simply survived the hard times can lift both your bank balance and your spirit. If there is someone you particularly admire, you could do worse than learning the secrets of their success from their biography or autobiography.

Mistakes

The hardest way to learn anything is also the best – learning from your mistakes. If you look at the list of Fortune 500 CEOs, most of them will have either been sacked at some point or been declared bankrupt. Failure is nothing to be scared of or embarrassed by. Certainly, venture capitalists are interested in backing companies led by CEOs with experience – even if that is the bitter experience of failure. That's because experience counts more than any qualification could. Many of our most successful business leaders never got their A-levels, let alone a degree or an MBA.

You can't gain experience without making the odd bad decision, embarrassing yourself from time to time, or visiting the darker ends of a few blind alleys. The secret is to learn from your mistakes and repeat them as rarely as possible. If you make a professional *faux pas*, don't lose sleep over it unnecessarily – analyze it. Were you unprepared, too eager or too mouthy? Perhaps you simply misread the situation. Whatever it was, as long as you can work out why it happened, you'll be well on the road to making sure it never happens again.

As a Free Agent, you'll be doing a lot of things for the first time – possibly using disparate skillsets and knowledge bases. Of course you won't be brilliant at everything first time round. Whenever you make a mistake, take heart from the fact that you're wiser now – if you hadn't made the error, you wouldn't know what to do if it happened again.

As well as your own mistakes, you can learn from other people's. It's a very arrogant Agent who thinks 'that'll never happen to me.' It's one thing making a mistake when it was unavoidable, but when history can teach you a lesson you should seize the chance to learn.

Use what you know

How many school children have complained, 'But when am I going to use algebra in the real world?'? It's a rhetorical question. Unlike many of the things you had drummed into you at school, almost everything you learn as a Free Agent is of professional value. So use it. You might feel dumb making mistakes, but not nearly as dumb as when making mistakes you really should have avoided.

tools three
selling

We're all sales execs now

Whatever your profession, as a Free Agent there is one tool you will use on a daily, if not hourly, basis – selling. You will be selling yourself – or your skills, or your products – with every call you make and at every meeting you attend. Whether you get work through recommendation or sweat through months of pitching, your sales skills will be the key to your success.

Contrary to popular belief, selling isn't about the gift of the gab or badgering people into submission. It's about applying some thoroughly tested principles to any situation. There's nothing magical about it – it's logical. Selling is not an art but a science, and consequently anyone can learn the basics.

This chapter will run through the techniques and practices of some of the most efficient and successful sales executives. They can be applied to selling yourself, your business or your products – and they can all be adapted to suit your situation.

Remember, selling is one of the essential mechanisms of commerce. It's not nasty, predatory or even particularly difficult; it's a transaction like any other. And just as it's your job to sell your services, it's someone's job to buy your services. Never feel like you're 'putting someone out' – you're just doing your job and trying to make it easier for them to do theirs.

Preparation

The first stage involves a lot of planning and mental preparation. Selling is about specifics – goals and targets – so it is not good enough to just get on the phone and call everyone you can think of. You should start with your personal requirements for Me plc. The fundamental starting point should always be – how much money do you need to earn? Then divide your annual salary by the amount you can charge for each piece of work or product. This will tell you how many times you need to successfully sell yourself each year.

To keep this simple, let's say you work out that you need to complete at least one 'sale' a week. ('Sale' means getting a piece of paid work, selling goods, or however you earn your living.) Now work out how many calls you have to make to secure the single sale. For argument's sake, let's say that you manage to turn one in four prospects (potential customers) into sales. That means that you need to call or see at least four prospects every week, assuming that each customer only requires one call for you to secure the sale. If they need two calls, then you'll have to make eight; if they need three, then you'll have to call twelve potential targets each week. If you don't put in those calls, then you will never make the sales and never make the money you need to survive. It's a very simple equation.

Your potential targets may be people you've known for years, worked with previously, or even friends – selling yourself to them may seem more daunting than pitching to strangers. But if you're going to run a successful Free Agency, you have to control the routes by which you find work and the easiest route is through friends. You might not see having lunch with a contact as a sales situation, but if you don't make the effort to make that lunch appointment, you are forfeiting a much needed sales opportunity. Selling doesn't just mean cold calling.

At this point you might be thinking, 'But I don't have time to do all that selling – I've got a business to run!' The trick here is to see selling as an integral part of what you do, not a daunting or difficult add-on. Like your tax return and chasing invoices, selling is essential. To think about it another way, there's no point making anything unless someone's going to buy it. A business without customers will never survive. As time-consuming as selling is, when you start a new business like Free Agency, it's as essential as it is unavoidable. Like laying foundations before you can build a palace.

Another thing to bear in mind is that selling gets easier and less time-consuming. Unlike a company that can take on staff or move to bigger premises and grow exponentially, you as a Free Agent cannot continue to take on job after job – there simply aren't enough hours in the day. This means that if you can hold on to clients and customers, you will have to find fewer of them as you get yourself established. You will still need the sales skills you will learn here though – as then the challenge will be to start persuading existing clients to pay you more!

There is another part to preparation – and that's mental readiness. Selling requires an agile, positive mind and sometimes – let's face it – we're not always in the mood. But there's a trick to getting in the mood. Now this might sound like magic rather than logic, but believe it or not this will really help you open doors, get calls returned and make sales …

You need to visualize your success.

Start seeing yourself as a winner. Whether that's imagining how every sale will go before you start or just seeing yourself at the next industry conference, talking amicably with several satisfied clients, imagining your success is a vital part of the process. To sell successfully you need to believe in what you're selling – and this will really help. It also prevents you from sounding desperate. Try it.

Love what you sell

This is crucial to making a sale. If you are not convinced about your abilities then you are never going to convince someone to pay you for them. So first of all you need to know your product (yourself or your skills), and then you need to love it. Every successful salesperson you will ever meet will truly believe in the products or services they sell. You must too.

Start off by listing everything you do or make. Then see what you do best. Is there anything you do better than anyone else? If you already have clients, speak to them about what they find easiest or best about dealing with you. Build up a clear picture of how your Agency is perceived and valued.

Think methodically about what you have to offer and what you can sell most easily. Is it your ten years at a blue-chip company, or the fact that you've just learnt the latest version of a piece of software? Is there anything you do that would impress a client – sector knowledge, constantly updating skills or the fact that you're fast or available 24 hours a day? You may want to refer to the asset list you made in the Are you a Free Agent? chapter.

Don't clutch at straws – make sure you are confident in your strengths and abilities. This list doesn't have to be endless (although you do want to be sure of the details). Imagine you're designing packaging for yourself. What you're working out here are the 'major sells', i.e. the reasons people will choose you over the guy on the next shelf.

Get to know your customer

It's much easier to sell to someone if you know what they want, so start researching your potential clients. You can only get to know someone when you know who they are. So even though you probably have a good idea about the first five or even ten people you're going to approach, start thinking about who else you can sell to. Because if they're not in need of your services this month, or are on holiday or too busy on something else to interview new suppliers, you might find that your first ten calls don't get you beyond the receptionist.

So start thinking *laterally* about who would pay you for your skills. You almost certainly know people in your primary market, but start investigating a secondary market for your talents. Identify a list of companies and clients that might need you. Then work out why they would need you – uncover their motive for hiring you. In business as in life, people only do things that benefit themselves. The key is to work out what they need most.

Often this is easy – a cheaper, faster or better version of what they've got now. Sometimes though, you might be selling to their vanity rather than their balance sheet. If you have a way of making them look good, that may be just as valuable – possibly even more valuable – than being cheaper than anyone else or incrementally increasing their profits. So don't think about what you sell, think about the benefits of what you're selling.

Always sell the benefits, not the product.

Once you get to know your customers, you will understand what aspects of your talents would benefit them most – this is what you'll sell.

Take time to do your research on clients. Sometimes the smallest nugget of information will be the lever that pushes the sale forward. So read extensively in your search for clients and motivations. Talk to your contacts and use your industry knowledge to work out *why* someone needs you.

The next step is to find out who to approach within any organization. Sending a letter to the wrong person is a waste of more than a stamp. Your extensive reading of the trade press will have given you the names of some players and the kinds of projects they work on. Your contacts might reveal some other names. Some industries produce directories of companies that may provide some useful first contacts for you. Beyond that you'll have to pick up the phone and ask to be put through to 'the person who deals with …'

The approach

Part of your research should involve finding out the best way people like to hear about your services. You will probably already know the industry standard procedure for your sector. Some companies never see reps, some people always require something in writing, and some just won't take you seriously unless you've got a glossy brochure. (For most Free Agents the glossy brochure is a complete waste of time and money. It's almost certainly a pretty distraction that gives you something to procrastinate about rather than getting on with the business of selling.)

You don't want to waste your resources or a potential client's by approaching them in the wrong way. Some people only open their mail once a week or are rarely at their desks and so never answer the phone. Emails are often too easy to delete. If you turn up at someone's office on spec, there's no guarantee they'll be in – or in the right frame of mind to see you. Sometimes you can get a better response just by targeting someone at a different time of the day or different time of year. So you see why determining the correct approach is important.

Often the best approach is a combination of all four. Maybe you give someone a quick call to let them know you're going to pop something in the post, or maybe you call them a few days after you sent an email to make sure they got the information. There are no hard and fast rules about the best way to approach new clients – except that you have to be prepared to try any and every way.

Questions first ...

Once you've got hold of the right person, try to discover what they need and why they need it. After you've politely introduced yourself, ask them how they usually use someone like you, if they're happy with the procedures or quality of work. Ask them what would be the most useful additional service someone in your position could offer. Never ever launch into a spiel or sales script. After all, you're just a friendly Free Agent who wants to help, not a hard-nosed sales rep flogging something the client don't want. And if you've done your research well, you will rarely approach the wrong person, therefore giving yourself the best possible chance of a positive reception.

You mustn't feel like you're wasting their time – although at times it might seem that way. You are trying to help them. By finding out their goals you can tailor your service for them. You might want the business, but you're still helping them.

Ask as many questions as necessary: How much do they spend in your area? Are they looking to expand, or to save costs? What are their priorities for the next quarter? For the next year?

… then start the sell

Once you've got a clear picture of what your client wants, when they want it and how they want it, you're finally in a position to start selling. You now know exactly what you have to offer to get the business – you are in a very good position. Hopefully, all you will have to negotiate is price. In reality though, even if you offer a better product or service, people are reluctant to change suppliers because they simply don't want to take the risk or they just can't be bothered.

This is where you remind them of the benefits switching to you will bring. Perhaps you're faster or nearer or easier to deal with. Don't start selling until you're sure you can give them what they've told you they need.

If they resist, repeat back their requirements to them stating that you've matched every one and exceeded some. Find out what their remaining objections are – it might be that they are just worried about the paperwork or something else you could offer to help with.

To recap then, there are essentially three parts to every sell:

1 **The Prelude**, where you outline everything they say they want or need. This is psychologically important – they know you've listened and are hopeful you will be the solution they're looking for.

2 **The Explanation**, where you reassure them that you offer everything they say they need or want. This is the meat in the sandwich, the bit they'll really chew over – so make sure you get it right.

3 **The Clarification**, where any objections are concerned or ironed out. Listen carefully to their objections – sometimes all people will want is to know that they've been heard. This is your chance to modify your offering to ensure you give them exactly what they want.

Now, all you've got to negotiate is the price!

The price

When you start putting a price on your services, take a moment to remember exactly what you're selling. You're not selling your time, your expertise or even your wares – you're selling a solution. Here's an example of how a solution is much more valuable than the Agent's skills.

A small publishing company was on the verge of going to the printers with their biggest ever order. It was a make-or-break situation for the company – if they missed the print run it would cost them thousands of pounds – and maybe hundreds of thousands of pounds in terms of loss of face with their client. They couldn't blow it. However, hours before deadline their server packed up. The MD was tearing her hair out, the publisher was shaking he was so scared of losing the money and the client. Thankfully, one of the employees had worked somewhere previously where they had used an emergency systems engineer who promised to be on site within the hour. They called him and told him the problem.

They asked him for a quote but he said he couldn't possibly put a price on the job until he saw the server, to which they agreed. An hour later he looked at the server and told them it would cost £5,000 pounds to fix. They had no choice but to agree.

The engineer sat down, pressed a few buttons and within seconds the server flickered back into life. The publisher couldn't believe that someone could charge £5,000 for less than a minute's work. Then he looked at the engineer's itemized bill:

Fixing the server	£5
Knowing how to fix the server	£4,995

Price, then, is not a concrete figure. Many unsuccessful salespeople think they would sell more if they could drop the price. Successful salespeople rarely think that price is an issue. Price is something that may rise or fall depending on the client. Often your fee for a piece of work will be agreed in consultation with your client. As long as you know what you need to earn from a certain job, and how much they need you, you will arrive at the appropriate price for the job. The key is *attitude* and *understanding*. If it's your attitude that you are worth what you're asking, you will transmit that to a client. If you take the time to understand their needs and objections, they will pay you to provide the solution they need.

tools four
pitching

The basics of pitching

Many companies offer contracts through a pitching process. Not every Free Agent will have to pitch, but it's becoming an increasingly common way of winning work, so it's definitely worth learning the basics. Pitching is an extension of the interview process where several people are shortlisted for an advertised vacancy.

The basic pitch scenario runs like this: a company decides it needs a piece of work done and contacts a small number of companies or Agents it believes would be good for the job. It briefs those companies on the work, its aims, scope and budget, either in person or via literature. A few weeks or months later the invited companies pitch their proposals. The company that makes the best pitch usually gets the job. Sometimes work is also put out to open tender – contracts are advertised in the trade press and written proposals are requested, but in this chapter we will deal with the more likely pitch situations Free Agents find themselves in. These will usually be trying to win small contracts following an initial introduction, or possibly trying to raise finance for your new venture.

The first step in any pitch is to get invited! If your contacts or sales leads get you over that barrier, being asked to pitch is a real shot in the arm, but no guarantee that you'll win the contract just the best shot you'll ever have at winning it. But it's a shot you'll never get if you don't network.

Understand the brief

Before you think about what you can offer any project, make absolutely sure that you understand the brief. The client offering the contract wants you to come back and pitch ideas and solutions that will make him look good, and to do that you need a clear understanding of what's required.

If you're asking for investment, the same rules apply: make sure you understand the sorts of projects your potential investor is seeking; find out what amount they typically invest and what they want in return for their investment.

Like everything else in business, the foundation of good pitching lies in good research.

These are the sorts of questions you need to ask clients when you intend to pitch for a piece of work:

- Why do they want this done?
- What are their ambitions for this project?
- What are the firm's overall aims for the project?
- In what spirit will the project be conducted?
- Within what boundaries will the project exist?

Remember to ask detailed questions about the specifics of the project, for example:

- What's the deadline?
- What's the budget?

- What's the target/threshold?
- How will the success be measured?
- What's the single most important element?

Ask whatever questions will give you the information needed to put together the best pitch you possibly can. Make sure you understand how the client wants to be pitched at – will they expect samples or a presentation? How formal will it be and how long will you have to make the presentation? Also check what technology they have for making a presentation – can you use their computer/projector/flip chart or will you need to bring your own?

Now go away and devise the best possible response to the brief. What you develop should help your client reach his aims and objectives, and include the best ways to hit the targets. Once you have developed your proposals, return to the brief to make doubly sure that you haven't missed something you were expressly asked to cover.

Presenting your ideas

From your point of view, the purpose of pitching is to prove to the pitchee that you are the most capable person to deliver for them or offer the best possible investment. Your presentation should convince them of this.

If you aren't going to be working alone on the project, bring any significant subcontractors (possibly other Free Agents) with you. If you are asking for investment, make sure every significant person in your team attends.

It's standard practice to give presentations on laptops, often in PowerPoint. But you can use flash cards, flip charts or an overhead projector – or you can do away with all props and just let them see the fire in your eyes. Don't waste time panicking about the medium you will use – concentrate on the message.

When preparing the slides or flash cards, break down your pitch into key elements and create a slide for each. There's little point just putting your speech up on the screen and then reading it out loud.

Make the medium work for you.

Use charts and photos, sales figures and research data – anything that looks good visually, and that makes you appear smart and authoritative, will have a greater impact than if you just read it out.

As a general rule, presentations should give overviews, highlights and examples of what you can offer – the detail will either be covered in a written document you leave with them or during a question and answer session after the presentation. If you're asked to give a quote or an amount you require for investment, leave it for the written document – don't put it up on a screen to be two feet high. It'll only remind them just how much it's costing them, and as we discussed in the Selling chapter, if the solution is right then the price shouldn't be a problem. If you are asking for investment, tell the pitchee exactly how and when they'll get their money back.

If you are using some kind of visual aid (PowerPoint, flash cards, etc.) make sure they look good. It's worth paying to get documents laser printed or logos scanned in. However, keep in mind that an expensive glossy cover won't get you the gig – you just want to create a professional image and remove the possible hurdle of 'Are they professional enough?'

Once you have your team, your visuals and a script, then it's time to rehearse – ideally in front of someone other than the mirror! Make sure your trial audience understands what you want them to understand of your proposals. Let them ask questions – you need to be able to respond to any little holes or mistakes they uncover. During your rehearsal, time yourself to check that your running time is within the allocation set out in the brief.

Giving a presentation

When you, your laptop and maybe your cohorts walk into someone else's office to give a presentation, be prepared for things not to go to plan. Maybe the boardroom was double booked and you've been moved to the canteen; maybe the projector's not working. When you're new at giving presentations it's easy to get thrown when things don't go as expected. Stay calm – you've still got some blinding ideas to show them. If you're not able to deliver what they're expecting (perhaps a member of your team is ill or your laptop is playing up), tell them straight away – be professional.

It's good practice to hand your business card to everyone in the room. If they've seen five other people for this particular contract, it will help them remember you. Once the hand shaking and greetings are done, take charge of the meeting. Say something like, 'If everyone's here I'll make a start' – that gives them a chance to stop you but makes you look efficient and keen. Then stand up or remain sitting – whatever seems appropriate or whatever you are most comfortable with.

A good structure for any presentation goes something like this:

1. Thank them for the opportunity to pitch.
2. Introduce yourself, giving a potted version of your CV and your suitability for the gig. It's always a good idea to mention how much you enjoyed working on the pitch and how excited you are about the project, even if you're not.
3. Run over the brief, demonstrating that you understand what they want from you.
4. Assure them that your ideas cover all the bases.
5. Run through your ideas, first in broad terms, then picking out some examples.
6. Include something memorable, something funny or something they've never seen before.
7. Hand the floor over to questions.

When giving your presentation, try to find a way of coping with your nerves. It's OK to be nervous – many experienced people never get rid of their nerves – but if you are too outwardly awkward it will detract from what you're saying. Speak clearly and naturally – make it seem like you're talking at them rather than giving a speech. If you don't mind being interrupted, say so; otherwise ask them to keep their questions until the end. It's very important to look at them (this is very easy when you're using a laptop or projector as they will be looking at the screen, just don't look away when they do change their focus back on to you as it will make you seem devious).

End your presentations by saying something affirmative like, 'I'm ready to take your questions now,' rather than a lame 'OK, that's it'. If there's more than just you giving the pitch, decide in advance who's going to answer the questions. Sometimes it's a good idea for one of you to 'chair' the session, directing the appropriate question to the appropriate team member. You want to avoid talking over one another.

At the end of your presentation, ask the potential client when they will be making their decision, not forgetting to add that you'd be very excited to take the work on! If they don't get back to you within the stated timeframe, don't be shy about calling them up. They made you a promise they didn't stick to – so it should be they who feel sheepish. This doesn't make you sound desperate – it makes you seem efficient.

tools five
negotiation

Negotiation is not war

Most of us are afraid of negotiating. That's largely because we have a narrow definition of the term. We see negotiation as something shown on the news, when opposing sides or nations never seem to get any closer to resolution. Well, negotiation isn't war – it's only a process that makes as many people as possible as happy as possible. It's a good thing, not a scary thing.

Negotiation is something you've been doing every day for years without even noticing.

If you tell your kids that they can only watch a video after they've done their homework – that's negotiation. When you tell your boss that you want time off in lieu of the extra hours you've recently put in – that's negotiation. Negotiation is just a route to the most amicable conclusion. It's nothing to be afraid of.

As a Free Agent you will find yourself negotiating in many more situations than a typical employee. Details in contracts, fees, deadlines, bonuses, pay rises, profit shares or pay-offs. From your terms and conditions to significant elements of major contracts, you will find yourself negotiating more and more, often in more formal situations. So it's essential to understand the psychology and mechanics of good negotiating in order to steer situations your way.

The first thing to get straight about negotiation is that it's not about 'winning'. You won't be taking anything that someone isn't prepared to give. Let's consider a very basic-level negotiation, say, buying a car. The dealer advertises the car at £10,000 but you only want to pay £7,500. Eventually you might get the car at £7,000 with a stereo thrown in. You may *think* you've driven a hard bargain, you may even *feel* like you've beaten the dealer into submission, but the truth is he hasn't sold you anything he wasn't prepared to sell you. You got the car, he got the sale – you both got what you wanted.

Successful negotiation is about win/win, not win/lose.

The following tools will help you get to win/win.

Prepare

All successful negotiations contain three main elements:

- preparation
- probing
- proposing.

Some contain a fourth element – persuasion – but this isn't always necessary. Preparation, as with almost everything in this book, is the foundation of success. Before you enter a negotiation, research your options and requirements thoroughly, as well as those of the people you're negotiating with.

Whether you're negotiating face to face or via email, start by devising your best-case scenario – all the terms and conditions you can dream of plus the fattest fee you've ever had the pleasure of invoicing for. Next, decide the absolute minimum you require to proceed with the deal. The difference between your best-case scenario and your absolute minimum is your negotiating range. The other side will have their range too – try to anticipate what their range is, because most settlements are found where both parties' ranges overlap.

As part of your preparations, also consider your alternatives, your Plan B. If we return to the car-buying scenario, this might mean buying a different model or using a different dealer if you don't get what you want. If you're in a salary negotiation, then having another job offer is the best possible alternative. The purpose of identifying your Plan B is that it gives you confidence when you're bargaining. It makes you an equal with whoever is on the other side of the table because you know you can walk away.

Perhaps the most important part of your research will be your investigations into outside factors that will influence the outcome. For instance, find out what the average pay settlements in your sector are, or how you can claim to be directly responsible for the growth of the company. Try to have any external factors that may affect the company, the project or the deal at your fingertips. This can be tedious, but it's as essential as turning up to the meeting.

Probe

Once you're in a negotiation, the next most important step is to ask as many questions as possible. The more you know about what the other side wants, how they want it and when they want it, the stronger the position you're in. Sometimes you just have to keep digging to find out exactly what the other side really wants. The more you ask, the more you understand. And – as knowledge is still power – the more you know, the more likely it is that you'll get to a satisfactory deal.

The most important aspect of probing is finding out 'why'. If for example, someone says the deadline is 12 May, ask them why. It might be an arbitrary date selected for convenience, or it might be because as soon as you have delivered your work they can complete another of their contracts. If it's the latter, you are in a strong position

– as long as you are sure you can meet the 12 May deadline. It's OK to start a negotiation not knowing all the facts, but by the time you actually start talking details you must have more information about the deal in your head than they have in theirs. So always remember to ask why.

The probing phase is important for another reason too: it gives the other side a chance to be heard. Often this is all some people want – to be heard, to be understood and to be taken seriously. Often, just by listening and sympathizing with the other side, you can diffuse any tension before it arrives. So ask, ask, ask, but never forget to listen, listen, listen.

Propose

Sometimes it can be beneficial to take a break between the probing and proposing phases of a negotiation as it can help you incorporate what you've learnt into what you offer. If possible, let the other side do the proposing first – if they're inexperienced they may launch into proposing before they've asked you any questions – this gives you yet more information, and therefore more control.

If the other side asks you to propose first, tell them that – as you're a flexible Free Agent who can accommodate a greater range of options – it would be expeditious for them to go first. That way you can respond to their demands. When you start to propose, make sure that you respond to the concerns you've uncovered during the probing phase. If you know their range, then you know what the minimum you have to propose is to reach agreement.

When you propose, don't reveal too much too soon. Start with the outline and seek approval for that before you move on to the details or secondary actions. If you can take them with you at each stage, you end up taking them with you to *your* conclusion, rather than their own.

When it gets difficult

For most Free Agents, negotiations are relatively straightforward as you are only representing yourself. You don't have a board or employees to worry about. However, keep in mind that many of the people you will negotiate with will have those responsibilities. It can be frustrating when you are in a position to move and the other side isn't, but then the real art of negotiation is simply controlling your nerves and your temper.

Being polite, understanding and courteous is the only way to build trust in negotiations. There's no point reaching agreement through attrition and argument if in the end you detest the sight of each other so much that you can't work together. At every stage, stay calm and remain confident – don't be the one to wobble.

If you keep coming unstuck at the same stumbling block, the trick is to break the problem down into its component parts. For instance, if the problem is the deadline, investigate why that deadline has been chosen. Look at all the factors that have helped determine the deadline they're trying to impose. It might be that dealing with one of those minor factors enables the deadline to become more flexible. This is true for most hurdles in most negotiations – it's the tiny details that have been unnecessarily allowed (usually through neglect) to cement into concrete barriers that prove tricky. But they are often easily dealt with once identified.

Some negotiations never reach the goal either party has in mind – the two sides are so intractable that compromise is the only solution. In most cases, compromise will come, but only after a great deal of time. If you find yourself in this kind of ongoing negotiation, look for the common ground and identify areas where you can co-operate immediately. Move towards the goal even if you can't reach it. Perhaps once you've worked together for a while the trust will have built to the level necessary to take the negotiation to the next level. There is always room to move somewhere.

Finally, it may be necessary to set a deadline for concluding a negotiation. Without deadlines some parties keep pushing agreement back. If you find yourself ready to move but the other side ignores this, impose a deadline. And back this deadline up with a penalty of some sort – either a financial one or a withdrawal of any previous offer.

The chances are that you will never find yourself in anything this protracted – after all, Free Agency is all about streamlining bureaucracy – but if you are prepared to negotiate hard, most of the time you will always get what you want.

David • 34 • gamer • London

David started taking his career seriously quite late in life. 'Guys I was at school with went to work from college and by the age of 22 or 23 were earning decent money. I was still working in a shoe shop.' As he started feeling envious of his mates' spending power, David made his first smart move as a Free Agent.

'I lived in Peterborough at the time and I knew from a mate who worked in the games shop – I was such a big Nintendo fan – that there was a guy in town who was building and designing his own games. The word was that he had just sold a game to a big American software company.' David got hold of his number and got in touch. The story about the American deal was true and he needed help to finish the new game in time.

'I just helped out round his flat, answering the phone and playing the new game looking for bugs. I really enjoyed my time working with Stu. It seemed like a really nice way to earn a living.' So David looked around for a business opportunity. 'I didn't know a thing about business – not a clue – so I just started buying and selling second-hand games. I advertised in *Loot* and gaming mags and I did quite well. My sister and her mates helped out on Saturdays, bagging up the games and getting to the Post Office on time.'

Suddenly he could outspend his old school friends and started to feel like he'd made it – a self-made man. Then the tax office got in touch. 'At first I didn't really understand what they wanted from me, but I slowly realized that I had no idea about running a business and it had never occurred to me that I'd have to pay tax.' After three years of blissful ignorance, David's tax bill was over £7,000.

After arranging a loan to cover his debt, David was starting to learn a little about business. He knew he could wheel and deal and also knew he was good at it. If he could learn the theory behind it all he thought he might have quite a good future. At 27 he went to university to read business studies. At the end of the three-year course his mail-order business had withered and he was even further in debt –

but he wasn't worried because he now knew he had the skills to get out of the mess he'd got himself into.

He approached Stu, who was still building games, and proposed going into business together. 'I thought we could sell his games directly – making use of his knowledge and my knowledge. We also started making use of the net, which was very slow back then but gamers were already online and loving it.' Stu eventually developed some new software that got big business interested. This was the day David had predicted would come, the reason he had studied business. 'I negotiated to sell the business for a hell of a lot of money – Stu and I both made several hundred thousand pounds each and we got jobs with the big company that bought us.' David moved to London, bought a few suits and started living the corporate life of the employee. It was the first 'proper' job he'd ever had. 'I couldn't believe how easy being an employee was – someone paid for me to have lunch, someone washed the mugs every night, they even paid for my taxi home!' He also kept getting bonuses as his ideas and negotiation skills kept pushing the business forward. 'It doesn't matter whether I'm running the company or on staff, I still behave the same. It seems to get results.'

tools six
flexibility

Learn to love change

Let's face it, if you were the kind of person that just wanted a quiet, predictable life, you wouldn't be a Free Agent. Inherent in being an Agent is the knowledge that everything is subject to change. Change is something you'll learn to expect, and to love. The trick is to incorporate change into every plan you make. The more flexible you can be, the more you will achieve as a Free Agent.

Change can come in many forms – your clients may change their minds, your suppliers may change their prices (up or down), stock markets crash, and priorities go in and out of fashion depending on your boss's mood. As a Free Agent you've got to be able to change direction instinctively.

Like a lone shark cruising the corporate ocean, you've got to dart in and out of opportunity faster than anyone else.

Very few projects or working days run as smoothly as you anticipate. Every day someone forgets something, someone is off sick or the server crashes – it's just part of life. And so you have to be able to deal with these often trivial setbacks.

The solution is to plan for them. When you are calculating how long a job will take – always add on another 10 to 20 per cent to allow for let-downs. If you have the luxury of incorporating delay or corrections into your timetable, you will deal with them far more efficiently. It's just good project management – you simply need to set aside time for change. Alternatively, always aim to bring projects in well before deadline. This way last-minute urgent requests won't send you into a panic. Another benefit is that if it's gorgeous weather you can take the day off without worrying about keeping your promises!

This might sound bizarre, but sometimes to be flexible you'll have to turn work down. If you're freelance this can be so difficult it's almost painful. But it's important that you leave time free to respond to new demands. If your back is up against the wall desperately trying to finish fifteen projects at once, then you're not going to be in a position to adapt. That means you don't keep your client happy or the work you produce is of less value in a changed market. Sometimes it's a false economy taking on extra work.

In other circumstances, change can affect cashflow and this requires another kind of planning. Like negotiation, change is easier to contemplate if you've got a back-up plan or alternative. Whether that's other work, having enough cash in the bank to see you through to the next contract, or the ability to walk away and go fishing for the next few years, just knowing there are other options available to you encourages you to accept and embrace change.

For some Free Agents, the cushion they need is having an alternative source of income – either from property, share dividends, syndication of their work or from the ability to switch clients easily. Having a secondary work for anything you produce is one of the best buffers you can have against the unexpected. You should also keep in mind that your contacts and reputation are your best defences against the negative aspects of change, as they will always bring fresh opportunity.

When change has a negative effect on your working plans, try and twist things to your advantage. A client might have just pulled out of a meeting, or a supplier might have just let you down: learn to view that as an opportunity. Perhaps to talk to your accountant or get a new insurance quote. Being let down isn't nearly so bad if you can make good use of the time – so make sure there's always something in your in-tray for you usefully to deal with.

Markets change

It's not just clients that change their minds and briefs that shift in the sands of time, markets change too. If you've been developing something that you were preparing to sell in a boom time, what happens if recession starts to bite? Or if your client becomes the subject of a takeover? There's not much you can do about it once it happens, but you might have been able to anticipate it. Your research should prevent you from facing too many surprises, but even if something does come out of the blue, your contingency planning should see you through.

Market change can affect you even when you're not working. Technology and other developments can leave you behind if you're not prepared to change. If a certain piece of kit becomes industry standard, then you've got to know how to use it. If suddenly everyone in your industry has to master a new skill, you have to learn that new skill too. Keeping your training up to date will allow you change ahead of the pack – this will create its own opportunities for you to exploit.

Job titles change

Often there's one thing that stops Free Agents from being flexible – their ego. They aren't prepared to work for someone whom they used to consider an underling. Or they're not prepared to get out of bed for less than £200 an hour. As a Free Agent, you've got to be able to work on a variety of projects in a variety of roles.

If you've previously enjoyed a senior role, it can be hard no longer having the influence you were used to. But that influence has been replaced by opportunity – it's only your inflexible mindset that's stopping you seeing the benefits. It doesn't matter if you were the boss on your last project but a gofer on this one – what matters is that you're learning and enjoying yourself while being paid. Don't let your ego pigeonhole you.

If you're a gun for hire, you should be able to shoot from any position.

With all types of change the key factor is your ability to respond quickly. The longer you spend in shock or moaning about being let down, the longer your rival has to take an advantage. Your willingness to be flexible will be a serious boost to your career.

Adam • 28 • musician • Bristol

Adam always knew he wanted to be a musician. As a teenager he was forever in bands, writing songs and making demos. While he always had the dream that one day he would get a recording contract and play Wembley, the reality was that music cost him far more than it ever earned him.

'The good thing about starting so young is that I always knew what trying to make it in the music industry involved. From driving to gigs to making demos to buying new guitar strings, it must be a more expensive hobby than flying!' says Adam.

At the age of 20 Adam was smart enough to realize that fame and fortune wasn't going to happen overnight and so he decided he needed a back-up trade. 'I was determined not to teach music. That phrase about those who can, do, and those who can't, teach, constantly ran through my head. I was also aware that teaching was becoming a really tough profession and I'd be marking homework or arranging choral evenings when I should have been working on my own stuff.'

So he looked around for a way of earning money that was complementary to his music. 'I plumped for book-keeping as it was something I could learn to a high standard in a short space of time. It is also paid well enough an hour so I could work fewer hours a week and still be able to pursue the music.'

After two years of working as a book-keeper for his local council, Adam had enough experience to go freelance. 'I made the decision that the book-keeping could work harder for me. So I started approaching local recording studios, record shops, music shops and venues – just about anyone in Bristol connected with the music industry.'

Working from home, Adam spent every morning doing the payroll, VAT returns and tax accounts for his clients, some of whom were small companies while others were individual musicians like himself. After a year he was earning as much in a week as he had done in a month at the council. But that wasn't the most valuable difference his new Free Agent status brought him. 'Suddenly I had the most fantastic contacts with agents, publishers, bands, studios and music shops. I got supplies cheaper, I got lots of support gigs and found engineers who would do demos for me in exchange for licking their books into shape.' He also got invited to parties, met other musicians and started moving in circles that could really help his career.

Although Adam is still not a multi-millionaire pop star – and as 30 approaches he's acknowledging that any future success will probably be as a writer or producer – his book-keeping has easily furthered his music career. 'I met my writing partner through the contacts I made doing the books, as well as the manager who has got some of our songs recorded by other artists. These two things alone have changed my life, without all the other benefits book-keeping has brought.'

Adam is still book-keeping, as well as writing music and playing in a band, hoping for his luck to change. 'The other guys in the band are always skint – they never got a trade to back up the music and so they're always in and out of jobs they hate. I don't like book-keeping very much, but it's a very solid foundation to have in a very volatile business.'

tools seven
imagination

Feel the joy

Some people have active imaginations, some don't. Those people who don't have any problem conjuring thoughts from the ether are more likely to enjoy being a Free Agent.

One of the greatest advantages of Free Agency is having the time and opportunity to think.

It's this thinking time – a luxury most workers don't have – that can propel your career from average to exceptional. While other workers are trying to breathe as shallowly as possible on rush-hour transport, Free Agents are in the park with the dog or in the bath with the rubber duck. It's no wonder then that many people have their best ideas after they become a Free Agent.

An imagination is an invaluable tool to a Free Agent for many reasons. First, it helps you see the big picture. If you can visualize how your cog fits into the big machine, you can develop a clearer idea of your usefulness, your power and your purpose. This prevents you from losing your way – or your rag.

Your imagination can also help you visualize your future. Now that you no longer have a career path mapped out for you by a company offering promotion after promotion, having a picture in your own head of where you are going can be a huge motivator.

Imagining your success is often a prerequisite of finding success. If you can see yourself as the Agent you want to be, rather than the agent you are, it helps you convey confidence when you meet new clients or employers. It gives you a sense of purpose, and if you can imagine yourself being even better at what you do, it will boost your confidence too.

Think before you do

Barring happy accidents, flukes and coincidences, it is almost impossible to do something unless you've thought about it first. Advances and discoveries are almost always founded on a hypothesis that has been carefully thought out. Your imagination, therefore, is a bridge to achievement. If you can't think of anything new to do, you are destined to do what you've always done.

Creative thinking also allows you to get out of a hole or find a solution to a problem.

Whichever way you look at it, you are limited only by your imagination.

So if you don't have a particularly vivid one, how do you play on the same field with happy dreamers?

First, make a commitment to allow time for thinking every day. Take five minutes, half an hour or just as long as it takes for your toast to brown to think about the options each day brings. It may be useful to learn a meditation technique to shut out distractions or you may want to make copious lists – eventually you'll learn the best way for you to Power Think. Short bursts of intensive thought are easier to incorporate into your day and are usually far more productive than daydreaming for an afternoon. You may need a visual aid for your

Power Think – like your diary – to use as a prompt. Look at everything in your diary or on your 'to do' list and just imagine how every meeting will go. Slowly you'll start to have ideas about improvements or additions you can make to pitches and projects, simply by forcing yourself to imagine something different.

Brainstorming

Different people's brains work in different ways. Not everyone has the ability to visualize or imagine, and you may find that even clearing time and space to think is not enough to let your imagination take off. In this case, replace imagining time with brainstorming time. Often the end result is the same: you just got there a different way. Brainstorming is nothing wild or difficult – it's simply a method of generating ideas that don't come naturally.

There are some simple rules that can help you get the most out of brainstorming, whether you do it alone or with someone else. First, create the right atmosphere – this means unplugging the phone, turning the radio off or telling colleagues not to disturb you.

Next make sure you have the right tools. You might want to try taping your brainstorming sessions, or just writing everything down. Some people find brainstorming easier if they make notes on a big piece of paper or a blackboard. Others like to put every idea on a Post-It ™ – that way they can move them around afterwards.

The next bit is the hardest for those whose imaginations don't work without the AA coming to jumpstart it, but if you are methodical the ideas will come. Now focus on the *purpose* of the brainstorm – whether it's how to find another job or how to sell coals to Newcastle. The trick is to write – or record – absolutely everything. Don't dismiss any idea because it's impractical or too expensive or too far-fetched. Most of us self-censor our thoughts and ideas far too quickly and it's vital with brainstorming to put every ridiculous idea down. If you are brainstorming with other people, don't judge their ideas, write them down too. The first stage of a successful brainstorm is utterly uncritical. Ideally this session should last for as long as useful suggestions keep coming. Generally an hour or so is enough – anything produced after that is often nonsense. If you don't feel you've had any decent suggestions, repeat this stage when you and/or your colleagues are in a different frame of mind.

Now you have your list, flip chart or tape of the brainstorm, leave it alone for an hour. Go and do something else, have lunch, whatever. Then try and remember some of the things on the list without looking at it. It's probable that you've remembered the best bits and this may well guide you in the right direction. Next, take a good look at your list with fresh eyes. There should now be several options in front of you that will either be a solution to the problem you were hoping to overcome, or at the very least the start of a solution.

You can repeat this process for the same problem, or start again with the results from the first session to see if you can work your ideas up to the next level. Brainstorming can sometimes produce hilarious results, far-fetched ideas and nonsense. Don't reject these ideas out of hand.

Many great inventions, companies and corporate leaders have become successful from daring to be different.

Innovation is the rocket fuel of industry, but fuel is useless unless you put it in your engine. So once you've got ideas, got suggestions or solutions, don't forget to use them.

MEET THE AGENTS

Jeff • 34 • media entrepreneur • London

'I can't wait for things to happen – I have to make them happen.' Jeff has all the energy and enthusiasm of the six-month-old puppy that accompanies him for most of his working day. He has his finger in more pies than an apprentice baker and is an expert at being a Free Agent. An Australian by birth and a TV journalist by training, about six years ago he made the decision to capitalise on both those facts.

He came to London with a new generation of broadcast-quality cameras. Like so many Free Agents, changes in technology were the catalyst for changes in his life. As a well-known face on Australian TV, he found it relatively easy to get a contract to file news stories back home. 'Suddenly news agencies started wondering why they were paying for a London bureau when one guy and a camera could do pretty much everything they needed.' He was dispatched all over Europe to cover stories from state visits to the cricket.

At the same time he started working for London-based agencies, editing other journalists' work. He soon started reporting for them too, but only on the basis that he kept the copyright on any of his work. This meant that he could sell it on to another news agency, as long as it broadcast in a different territory from the first. If he was smart, and lucky, he could get paid several times for the same piece of work. It also meant that he didn't have to do as much work as he used to. Sometimes just one story a month was enough to live on.

This freed up time for his imagination to lead him down new paths. It also gave him time to take care of his wife, cook wonderful meals, take the dog for long walks and enjoy an enviable lifestyle. He made plans for a documentary, wrote a book, and life was almost good enough for him not to miss the Australian sunshine.

His real leap into entrepreneurship came with the internet. Here, he realized, was an opportunity of a lifetime. 'The news industry spends a fortune on satellite transmissions and I realized that sending stories over the internet was cheaper.' He decided to start an online bureau for independent journalists who work remotely, like him, all over the world. They could send him their footage and he would package the reports and upload them to a website. News agencies around the world could then see the reports online and buy them. As desktop editing equipment was now good enough and cheap enough, it was possible for him to do all this from his spare room. So he's happy – and the puppy still gets lots of attention.

'The secret,' he says, 'is to exploit what you know and who you know. I've just played to my strengths. Another factor, I think, is that I've made use of technology as soon as it came along in order to keep my advantage.'

tools eight
determination

Keep the faith

When you work for yourself it can be hard to keep your focus, your momentum and your spirits up. If you haven't got colleagues around you all pulling in the same direction, it's easy to lose your way. When you have a bad day there's no one to take you to lunch, and when you have a quiet day there's no one to fill the gaps. One of the problems with Free Agency is that your working day is only as stable as you are. Your bad days can become catastrophic when there's no one around to provide balance and good humour. All Free Agents have to look inside themselves to find focus, strength and determination to keep on an even keel.

The buck stops with you: Free Agency is not for the weak.

As a Free Agent, you'll need all your determination and personal resources to see yourself through bad days. When you're bored, distracted, tired or ill, only determination will see you to the stage where you can prepare another invoice.

You have to be your own mentor, motivator, cheerleader and disciplinarian. When you make a mistake, you will have to comfort and support yourself. When you're lost, you'll have to be your own navigator. A Free Agent without determination floats like a seed on the wind with no control over whether they find fertile or fallow ground.

Sources of determination

There are a few simple tricks you can learn to keep your determination levels high enough to cope with everything from major crises to general tedium. The first trick is to visualize the successful outcome of every situation and project. If you can smell the success in the future, it's much easier to taste it in the present. Conversely, if you spend time worrying about completion and poor quality, this will allow your mind to wobble dangerously on to the unmotivated wayside. Imagining your goal, being able to see it, makes it much easier to head towards it.

Another trick is to break problems down into their component parts. Don't let one tiny problem prevent you from enthusiastically completing the rest of the project. You might be feeling down about an entire project or company just because of one difficult person, or one tricky meeting. In your mind, isolate the problem – this will have the effect of making it smaller and more manageable. Sometimes, when you identify and isolate the aspect that's upsetting your balance, it can seem trivial and ridiculous, and this really helps you to regain perspective.

If you're working on a huge project and you find yourself lost and unsure, it's a good idea to combine both these techniques. First, keep the end result in mind. Next, break down each challenge within the project and make a list or spreadsheet of each task. As you complete each stage you can tick off each success and calculate how much further you have to go. This list acts as a map to guide you through to the end and prevents you losing momentum and heart. As you near the end, your determination to finish the project will soar. But if you don't know where you are in a project, you can feel swamped and begin to lose heart.

Dealing with disappointment

Your ability to cope with knock-backs will be one of the characteristics that marks you out for success. When you're let down, when you screw up or when you get doors shut in your face, remember that everybody gets let down sometimes. You may as well accept now that every so often you're going to be dealt a bad hand, make a mistake or not be anyone else's priority. That's just the way it is sometimes.

There's no point moaning about bad luck. It doesn't help. Give yourself a break. You're allowed to fail from time to time. And just like sometimes shit happens, some days you simply won't have the energy to deal with it. And that's OK too. This book is about becoming a Free Agent, not a superhero. You don't always have to be capable and strong, so don't beat yourself up about it.

If you are in a position to cope with a knock-back, working out what went wrong and deconstructing the process that led to the disappointment can often prevent mistakes from repeating themselves. This is positive action. Whenever you can, take the energy from a negative event and catalyze it into positive action. It's much easier to be determined when you're feeling positive.

Find a mentor

The proverb says that a problem shared is a problem halved. Having someone to talk to about your career and your problems can be a tremendous fillip in troubled times. While it can help to talk to your partner and your friends, it might be more beneficial to talk to someone outside your social circle.

A mentor might be the answer. A mentor is someone who can advise you on your business, your contacts, your work and your future. They don't have to be senior to you or even work in the same sector;

they just have to be someone who has the time to listen and something constructive to say. A mentor can motivate you, give you perspective and support you. Having a mentor can help get you focused on your goals.

Some recruitment agencies also offer mentoring services, but as they're not cheap (anything up to £25,000) a year, it might be worth approaching someone you trust and asking them to be your mentor. This may be an old boss, an old lecturer – anyone who doesn't see you as a competitor. If you're wondering what the mentor gets out of the relationship, just imagine what an ego boost it would be to be asked, and then to have some smart ambitious professional hang on your every word. And if they're smart, they'll know that what goes around comes around and at some point there will be a favour you can do for them.

If you can't find a mentor, why not find another Free Agent you can hook up with from time to time? Perhaps you can help each other and prevent knock-backs from turning into fatal blows to each other's careers. Anything you can do to stay positive will help keep your determination levels high. You don't always have to do it on your own, but you must be capable of absorbing the odd blow. Remember, determination is just a confidence trick.

Janie • 36 • pr manager • London

After graduating with a degree in marketing in her early 20s, Janie followed a fairly standard career path in marketing. Every couple of years she either moved or got promoted until she found herself on a nice salary, with nice clients in nice West End offices. 'I was a typical career girl – Dorothy Perkins suits with expensive accessories! I loved the work and I loved the perks. I felt very lucky to be doing something I enjoyed.'

Janie married at 30 and immediately planned to start a family. 'My husband worked in electronics in the kind of position it's impossible to do from home, so we had always discussed me going freelance. But not until I had got my maternity leave!'

They stuck to the plan. Janie had her first baby while still employed, entitling her to her company's generous six months' maternity leave. She was able to use some of her time at home to prepare for going freelance before returning to work to fulfil her contractual obligations. Her mother-in-law looked after the baby when Janie went back to work – on the condition that it was a temporary arrangement. 'After three months back I resigned and left shortly afterwards – taking a client or two – to work from home.' Clearly, Janie is a very organized woman. Even her babies get born exactly when she plans!

For the next five years, Janie balanced being a mum with her fledgling PR business. 'Most of the work could be done from home. I needed my husband and mother-in-law to help out from time to time when I had to pitch for work or meet clients, but mostly it was sitting on the phone or preparing presentations on the PC.

'I was very careful about the amount of work I would take on as there was no point earning money that would go straight to a childminder – the whole point of this move was to be there for the kids and save childcare costs.'

Her family and her business both continued to grow (two kids and 14 clients) and Janie was very happy. 'Sometimes I just wanted to get out of the house, to get away from the mess. And sometimes of course the baby would start screaming while I was on the phone to an important client, but mostly it was an arrangement that worked very well. I really liked being my own boss.'

However, a dream opportunity arose as the PR manager for a respected City firm and she decided that it was worth going for. 'At the interview my chief exec asked how I would find being an employee again. I told him it wouldn't be any different – the work would still be the same, it's all clients, objectives and deadlines.'

After three interviews she was offered the job. 'I had decided that I wasn't going to give up my nice lifestyle easily and decided only to take the job if they agreed to my conditions. I told them I wanted to work a 35-hour week in four days rather than five. I also told them that I wanted to work from home for one of those days.' They agreed.

'To this day I don't think the chief exec knows which days I'm in the office and which days I'm at home, he just knows that I'm always there for meetings and my work is more than satisfactory. I don't think he likes the fact that I negotiated this package, but he likes having a hard negotiator as his PR manager, so everyone's happy.'

tools nine
decision making

It's up to you

No one tells a Free Agent what to do. From the time you start work, to how much work you do, to the kind of work you do, all the decisions are down to you. You can't afford to prevaricate any more and procrastination has to fly out the window.

As a Free Agent you have to learn to make good decisions, often at speed.

And while most decisions are actually very easy because the right choice is so obvious, sometimes you have actively to seize control of even the simplest decision. For instance, if you keep saying yes to every bit of work that you get offered, you may end up too busy to take on the big juicy contract that could turn your fortunes around.

Most people like to deal with decision makers. If you get a reputation as a ditherer or someone who doesn't stick to their word, it's bound to affect the amount of work you get offered. If you can make a quick decision – and stick to it – you make things easier for those around you, as other bits of the project may rely on your commitment. But before you get too panicked about the responsibility of it all, here's the good news …

Decision making is one of those skills we acquire naturally over time. Just the experience of life and work teaches us what we're capable of in a given amount of time, or the sorts of jobs that make us happy. We learn from making bad decisions, we learn from other people's examples – we just learn. The ability to make good decisions comes with wrinkles. But if you can learn to take good decisions earlier, you can give yourself a headstart.

The other good news about decision making is that it's pretty straightforward. When opportunity knocks, you should normally open the door and embrace the chances it brings. We don't learn much from standing still; indeed, many a false step is made by standing still. For most of us, most decisions end up with us saying 'yes'. The rest of this chapter will help you when things get a bit trickier.

Know yourself

The best way to making good decisions is by having as much information available to you as possible. So the first step, yet again, is research. You need to be sure of what resources you've got available in terms of time, supplies, ability and inclination. For a Free Agent, the most important resource is usually time. So it's always important to know how much of the stuff you've got on your hands. Get to know your diary and your commitments off the top of your head.

Every so often it pays to take an inventory of your skills, supplies and availability. Then you can determine if you've got what it takes to do the job. If you haven't got the resources, then you should say 'no'. And you should say 'no' as soon as you can – everyone appreciates a straight decision, even when it's not what they want to hear. Free Agents rarely like saying 'no' – especially if they're turning down work – but you can't avoid saying it at some point, it's just part of being free. If you really do have a problem with the N word, imagine you're back in your old job when someone asked you to do something you really, really didn't want to do and you weren't allowed to turn them down. At least now you're free – and the compensation for missing out on the work you're about to turn down is that at least it's your decision.

If you have sufficient resources, all you have to do now is decide if you want the work or not. This isn't necessarily the easy bit – especially if you're lucky enough to be mulling over a few offers. Sometimes we want to accept an offer because we feel obliged, or because we think it will be good for us. Sometimes there are clients that you never want to let down. If your emotions get in the way, try and look at your choices objectively. Imagine that a friend has asked you for your advice with the same dilemma – what counsel would you offer? If you're really in a pickle, then take a bit of time. Ultimately everyone prefers the right decision ahead of a quick one.

When you really can't decide

Sometimes decisions turn into dilemmas that have no simple resolution. If you find yourself in this situation, you must first tell whoever is waiting for your decision that they're going to have to wait. Ask them how long you've got to make your mind up. If they don't give you a deadline, give yourself one: if you let the decision-making process go on too long, it will take time and energy away from more positive aspects of your Agency.

Next, break down each decision into mini-decisions. Find the component or components that are proving to be the sticking points. See if there is some way that these elements can be eliminated or ironed out. Just the process of identifying and isolating them can help you identify ways to deal with them.

While you should always avoid saying 'maybe' (it rarely does anyone any favours), it's still possible to make partial decisions. You might not be in a position to commit to a final solution immediately. In this case, get back to the proposer and tell them that you can only take on some of what they want but not all, or that you can't start on the date they've asked for, or can't complete until a later date. If this is unacceptable to them, then you can either reconsider or walk away. If you're in this position it's probably because you have several other irons in the Free Agent fire, so this shouldn't be too hard.

If a little negotiation doesn't get you to a position where you can confidently make a decision, then you have a few more choices: you can trust your gut instinct, you can ask a friend, or you can even toss a coin. If you are still really, truly unsure, it might be that you know deep down that the opportunity is not right for you. Often if you have this much trouble saying 'yes' there's a good reason for it.

One final piece of advice: a useful guide for making a sound decision is doing things for the 'Greater Good'. If you have the foresight to do something now that might benefit you in the future, or the ability to see your short-term inconvenience as a benefit for someone in need; then more often than not you will feel like you've made the right choice.

Don't dwell on past mistakes – learn from them.

Find out what you should have done differently (possibly more research, or negotiated harder) so that you won't make the same mistake again. If you can learn from every choice, then you can never make a 'wrong' decision, only a poor one. And everyone can live with that once in a while.

MEET THE AGENTS

Jack • 62 • cabinet maker • Dorset

At 55, Jack retired early from his job in the Australian civil service organizing visits and press trips for successive administrations. His work had seen him close to the centre of power, enjoying plenty of overseas travel and a high standard of living. It in no way prepared him for the next chapter in his life. His partner was British by birth and was forced to return to Britain when her parents became ill. 'Our kids were old enough to take care of themselves and we were in a position to make the move. So we came.'

It soon became clear that Jack's pension wouldn't stretch as far in Britain as it had 'down under', and so he looked around for a supplementary income. 'There wasn't much obvious opportunity in rural Dorset to do anything other than open a shop. The big decision was deciding what to sell.'

Jack decided he wanted to indulge his hobby of woodwork. He set about making CD racks, shelf units and other small items from wood he reclaimed from skips. He then bought other items – like candles, birthday cards and dried flowers – from wholesalers to pretty up the shop. He priced items at what he calls 'impulse prices' and made sure everything was small enough to fit in the boot of a car. He knew most of his trade would be from walkers and tourists stopping off at the café next door.

'I didn't like running a shop, it's lonely and thankless, but it was an income and I needed money. What I liked about it was getting the chance to work with wood. Planing and working wood fills me with a really simple – no primal – happiness and contentment. I also really liked the fact that I had completely changed my life – from one hemisphere to another, from politics to woodwork. Anyone who thinks of retirement as more of the same is setting themselves up for boredom.'

Over time, Jack found himself acquiring regular customers. 'They enjoyed my furniture as much as I did and they started asking if I would make bigger pieces – mirrors, tables, wine racks and the like. I'd never made anything that complicated before but I had a go and they bought whatever I made.' Looking back Jack realizes he undersold his early pieces because he didn't think the work of an unskilled craftsman was worth it. 'But they loved it – in many cases I could have doubled the price and still made the sale.'

The real breakthrough in his new business came when his daughter and her boyfriend visited from Australia. 'They'd spent a few days in London before coming to Dorset and had been to Camden Market and Portobello Road and when they saw my stuff they said I could clean up in London.' After a couple of recces, Jack thought he could too and took a stall at Camden for a couple of days.

Instead of simply making more furniture and working longer hours, not to mention travelling to London once a week, Jack decided to set up a franchise with a stallholder in Camden. 'I sold him a couple of designs that he could make himself. He keeps the profit from those while acting as a teaser for my catalogue that shows what I make in Dorset. Customers can then place orders online via the website that my son's mate built in Australia for next to nothing!'

Jack took on an apprentice to help him with the orders but soon realized that he hated being a boss as much as he hated running a shop. So he got rid of the apprentice and sublet the shop to which he now supplies his furniture at guaranteed rates. 'If something doesn't sell it's not my problem any more. I don't traipse to London where the hotel cost wipes out any profit. I just sit in my garage doing what I love, stopping for an occasional smoke whenever I like to remember my mates in their non-smoking Canberra offices just waiting to have heart attacks.'

tools ten
time management

Time: the most precious commodity

An important reason for becoming a Free Agent is to gain more control over your most precious resource – your time. As the saying goes, no man is ever rich enough to buy back his past – it truly is a resource none of us should squander. Those who are in control of how they spend their time will be among the most contented souls on the planet.

Free Agency is a chance to seize control of your schedule and get happy.

If you can manage time, you really can do anything. It's one of the most powerful tools you will ever use – and it's a weapon few workers can utilize. Time management gives you an enormous advantage in work, as in life.

There is no 'right' way to time manage – you just do what works for you. There are some tips and suggestions in this chapter, but they're all virtually useless unless you know what you want. Good time management starts with seeing the big picture / the far horizon / the total gameplan. Time management is not just about bringing projects in on time (although this is important), it's about pacing yourself to make sure you hit your targets on time, or even ahead of schedule. Once you have worked out what your personal ambitions and goals are, you can then establish the rhythms and techniques you need to employ to help you achieve your aims.

It might be important to you that you never work beyond 3 pm. Or perhaps retiring at 40 is your goal and you're happy to work 24/7 until then, but not at all afterwards. Or it might be that you're really not a morning person and have never performed well before lunch. Whatever you discover, now is your chance to determine how you work best and when. So for time management, read life management.

As well as the long-term goals and targets of time management, there are the short-term ones. Although these are often smaller hurdles, they are trickier to plan for. The short-term tools set out below will let you accurately estimate how time consuming any given piece of work will be, and the long-term tools will ensure you get the right life/work balance for you.

The first step for both long- and short-term time management is determining how much time you have. No, this doesn't mean estimating when you're going to die! It means working out what existing commitments you already have.

Your family and friends need you for some hours of the week. You might go to the gym several times a week or follow your team to all corners of the country each weekend. It's very important for Free Agents to recognize and itemize these commitments – otherwise it's all too easy to lurch from one gig to the next leaving no time for life in between. As well as existing commitments, think about the other activities you would like to make time for. Being a Free Agent is about getting satisfied, so mark off time in your diary that you can dedicate to the pursuit of new pleasures.

The next step in short-term time management is knowing how long individual tasks take you. If you're experienced at what you do, you will have a rough idea of how long you will need to research a certain topic, how many phone calls you will need to make to achieve a certain target, or how long it takes for you to make your wares. Take some time to ascertain how long everything you do takes. This is something you will intuitively get better at the longer you work. If you're not sure, break each gig down into micro-tasks and estimate how long they will take you. If you build up from the length of each phone call, you will be able to come up with a reasonably accurate timeframe. You now have the background information to help you plan any project successfully.

Project management

The most important aspect of short-term time management is accurately estimating how long it will take you to finish a piece of work. If you're working on a small, straightforward piece of work, you will probably be able to determine from the brief whether it's a few hours' work or a few days' work. All you then need to do is to factor in your personal commitments – and any existing professional ones – and you can reach a likely deadline.

For more complicated pieces of work and larger projects, time management skills become more relevant and allow you to manage all your projects efficiently. The trick with large projects is to break them down into component tasks. Once you have done this, you need to determine the order in which those individual tasks have to be completed. For instance, there's no point ordering supplies until you know you've secured the contract. Some tasks simply can't start until others have been finished.

There are many templates you can use to manage projects, and many different pieces of jargon you can use to describe them (Gantt charts, work streams, critical paths). They all basically do the same thing – display the project as a series of tasks to be completed in sequence by certain dates. Take a look at the simplified chart that follows:

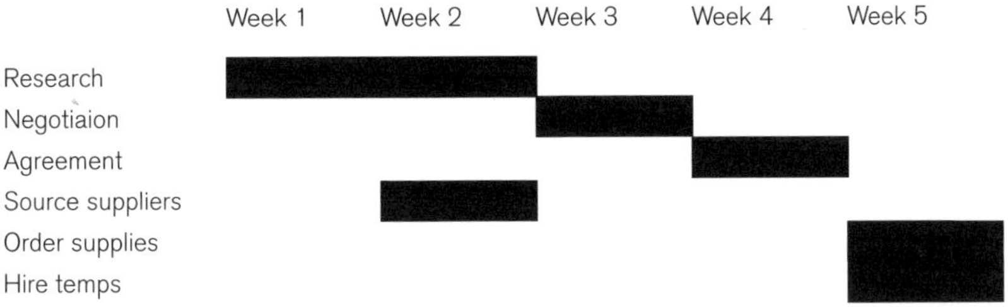

You can see from this chart that the research will take two weeks and that the negotiation cannot start until the research is finished. Agreement cannot come before negotiation and there's no point ordering supplies or staff until you have agreement. Colour-coded sequences are usually referred to as 'work streams', where the completion of one task is the trigger for the start of the next. If you operate such a chart on a standard spreadsheet, you can easily have supplementary sheets for each task – in this example that might be breaking the research down into mini-tasks or individual phone calls.

When you are determining deadlines and timescales, always allow a contingency in case you get sick. Most project managers allow a 10 per cent contingency on time and 20–50 per cent for budget. Allowing a little slack will help you to stick to the deadline. And if the project you're managing is running long term, don't forget to allow yourself some holiday time.

Once you have determined how long a project will take, it's vital to communicate the final deadline – and all the mini-deadlines in between – to everyone affected by them. There's no point working towards a deadline if others are working towards a different one.

Put the kettle on

Once you've determined the big and little pictures for your career, you need to get microscopic and take a careful look at your working day. It's very easy to get distracted when you've got to go to the post office, talk to the bank and pay the gas bill. And if you work from home, it's often too easy to take long baths and watch daytime TV. So you need to make sure you can control the distractions that might prevent you from working.

If you were working in an office, you would probably spend less that half your allotted hours actually working. The rest of the time is spent talking to colleagues, waiting on hold, walking over to the fax machine or waiting for people to turn up to meetings. So you don't need to be at your desk at 9.30 am and work solidly until 6 pm to get a full day's work done.

If you work for five or six hours as a Free Agent you're probably doing more than most PAYE workers per day.

The key thing here is not to put off the distractions, but to incorporate them. There are no rules on how to do this, but it might help to designate half an hour a day to domestic tasks, another half-hour for administration. If you don't timetable these chores they can seriously affect your concentration as they offer distractions from your real work. If, once you've finally got down to business, you find concentration on the task in hand difficult, try breaking it down and give yourself lots of mini-deadlines throughout the day. That way you constantly get a sense of achievement that helps keep you motivated.

If you need long stretches of time to get into the swing of the day or the project, once you get to know your working rhythm you'll know the times when you should schedule meetings. If you work from home, leaving to have a lunch meeting can be incredibly disruptive – so think about either getting your meetings out of the way first thing or leaving them until the end of the day. Alternatively, you may want to allocate a whole day for meetings to leave the rest of the week free.

If you're one of those people who finds concentration easy and your domestic or other duties can be forgotten from one month to the next – you have even more of a reason to timetable in some time every day for chores. However you work, learn your natural preferences and go with them. If you're not a morning person or you like to work seven days straight and take five off, then start building your diary to play to your strengths. Make the Free Agent advantage work harder for you.

Finally, however you work it's important to take breaks, if only to prevent repetitive strain injuries (RSI). A break can give you perspective and clarity, a chance to breathe deeply and reflect on the project. Taking five minutes now could save you days of wasted energy later. So put the kettle on.

tools eleven
money management

Don't worry

Many people never become Free Agents because (a) they're worried about the money coming in or (b) they're worried that they'll worry about the money coming in. Experienced Free Agents who have learnt to manage their cash flow hardly ever worry about money. You won't either.

We covered the basics of Free Agent money management in the Can you make it as a Free Agent? chapter. To recap, this involves making sure you have enough money to see you through until the first cheque arrives. You also need to give yourself a contingency budget. Do a bit of worst-case scenario planning – what happens if your client goes into receivership or your invoice goes astray? You need to make sure you have a slush fund that can cover you in emergencies. It's a good idea to keep your contingency money in a separate account – that way it's harder to spend it without thinking. Now we'll move on to managing your money on a monthly basis.

Even though you may no longer have a salary, most people still do and consequently most bills still come in monthly sizes. This means you need to amalgamate your cheques and fees into a monthly income. So whether you do 100 transactions a month at £20 a go, or

two pieces of work a year for £10,000 each, you need to work out your monthly average income. Treat this figure as your salary and spend accordingly.

Clearly it's essential that your monthly income exceeds your monthly outgoings. If it doesn't, you need to take immediate charge of your finances – either cut your cloth accordingly or hustle for more work. If you're heading for broke there's one thing you can't afford to ignore – that's the maths.

Tax, VAT and allowances

If you're a UK employee, you'll be used to getting a monthly payslip that tells you how much you've earnt that month, how much tax you've paid and what your National Insurance contributions are. It will also tell you how much tax you've paid for the year to date.

When your income comes from several sources, you don't have the benefit of being handed such a ready reckoner, so you have to make one. This will enable you to set aside the right amount of tax, VAT (if you register for it) and NI contributions.

To do this you must consult your last tax statement or call your tax office. You need to find out what your personal tax-free allowance is (the 2001–2002 standard is £4,535). Once you earn over your tax-free allowance, you pay 10 per cent tax on the first £1,880, and 22 per cent on the next £27,519. Any earnings over that are taxed at 40 per cent (again, for 2001–2002, check the current rates at www.ir-online.gov.uk). Now all you need to do is keep a simple record of all your income and expenses to find out what your taxable income is each month (that's the money earned minus any allowable expenses). This enables you to set money aside for your tax bill which you will pay after the end of the current tax year.

Here are a couple of examples of how to work out how much tax to put aside, assuming the worker has a tax-free allowance of the standard £4,535 and makes no charitable donations eligible for gift aid (this is just a guide). The tax to pay is in bold:

Example 1

Year to date

Earnings	*Expenses*	*Taxable income*	*Less allowance*	*Tax to pay*
£5,800	£600	£5,200	£4,535	10% of £665 = **£66.50**

Example 2

Year to date

Earnings	*Expenses*	*Taxable income*	*Less allowance*	*Tax to pay*
£39,000	£2,500	£36,500	£4,535	10% of £1,880 = £188
				22% of £27,519 = £6,054
				40% of £2,566 = £1,026
				Total tax = £7,268

If you update your own spreadsheet each month with your income and your expenses, then it's easy to keep track of the amount of tax you need to put on one side. And if you put your tax in a high interest account, you can also make money on it before you hand it over! You also need to pay your National Insurance contributions and it's easy to do this monthly by direct debit (just speak to the Contributions Agency).

If you register for VAT, keep similar records of how much VAT you charge and how much you are charged to make sure you know how much your VAT bill will be (unless of course you're due a rebate). VAT is currently paid quarterly in arrears, although the Chancellor is simplifying VAT rules for small businesses and sole traders. Again, if you put your VAT to one side, you can gain interest on it before you hand it over.

Make the banks work for you

As well as paying you interest on money that PAYE workers never see, your bank can also help you in other ways. There are now many products on the market that can greatly benefit Free Agents and by shopping around you can find some neat ways to manage your outgoings to better suit your incomings.

While few landlords will accept irregular rent payments, many lenders now offer flexible mortgages. These allow you to make supplementary payments when you're flush or take payment holidays when you're skint or having unpaid leave. These arrangements were devised for Free Agents but be warned – they usually come with higher interest rates than standard mortgages.

It might help you to open several accounts – and as most banks offer charge-free current accounts, you can do this at no extra cost. Some Free Agents find it easier to put all their income into one account (Account A) from which they transfer a monthly 'salary' into a second account (Account B) from which they make all their household and personal payments. This helps you stick to your monthly average income and prevents overspending on good months, leaving enough to see you through lean months. It's worth seeing what deals your bank offers you on overdrafts – if it's a free service, arrange one for each account for extra flexibility.

Over time, if there is more money in Account A, you can calculate a monthly pay rise for yourself, or you can transfer a lump sum to a savings account. Alternatively of course, you can spend it!

The best thing you can do with any excess money is to invest it. In yourself. Empowering yourself with new skills, new technology and new knowledge is the best investment any Free Agent can ever make – it will pay far greater dividends than just about anything else.